WORKING
with
Social
Research

WORKING
with
Social
Research

Sotirios Sarantakos
Charles Sturt University, Australia

First published 1998 by
MACMILLAN EDUCATION AUSTRALIA PTY LTD
627 Chapel Street, South Yarra 3141

Associated companies and representatives
throughout the world

National Library of Australia
cataloguing in publication data

Sarantakos, S. (Sotirios), 1939– .
    Working with social research.

    ISBN 0 7329 4894 0 (set).
    ISBN 0 7329 4893 2.

    1. Sociology – Methodology. 2. Sociology – Research. I.
    Sarantakos, S. (Sotirios), 1939– . Social Research 2nd ed.
    II. Title. III. Title: Social Research 2nd ed.

301.072

Typeset in Times by
J&M Typesetting Pty Ltd, Blackburn North

Printed in Hong Kong

Contents

Preface

While teaching research methods at a number of tertiary institutions in Australia and overseas, using initially British and American texts, I had the opportunity to teach students of diverse ethnic and academic backgrounds, and to gain an understanding of the difficulties they experienced while studying this course. This helped me to become aware of the specific needs of these students, to identify the study areas that required more elaboration and to adjust my teaching accordingly.

Apart from this, working with these students proved to be particularly useful when preparing *Social Research*. Most deficiencies identified by students in the texts used previously were eliminated, and the suggestions they made for changes, additions, adjustments and improvements were – where possible – incorporated in this text.

Nevertheless, many proposed additions could not be accommodated in *Social Research*. Some suggestions were beyond the physical boundaries of the book, while others were beyond the educational and intellectual scope of a text. This obviously left a gap in the teaching of the subject – a gap that lecturers met by providing their own support material.

The purpose of this workbook is to fill this gap. In its nineteen chapters – matching the number of chapters of *Social Research* – the book offers useful advice and assistance, which aim to make the study of this text easy and effective. Each chapter contains the following sections: contents, educational objectives, main points, short-answer questions, multiple-choice questions and practical exercises.

The list of *contents* offers an overview of the issues addressed in the chapter and outlines the boundaries within which the discussion will be developed. The *educational objectives* spell out what students are expected to learn and the goals they should work for. The list of *main points* gives a brief but comprehensive summary of each chapter.

Short-answer questions address the central issues of the chapter and help students to review its material. *Definitions of concepts* are set to motivate students to review the main concepts introduced in each chapter. *Multiple-choice questions* and *true/false questions* in the first thirteen chapters provide an opportunity to review some major aspects of the chapter's theme from a different perspective. In Chapters 14–19 the nature of the issues discussed and the limited space of this book did not allow for additional questions of this type. Instead, more extensive *practical exercises* are given.

Practical exercises in Chapters 3–19 provide an opportunity to apply, in real situations, the concepts, methods and techniques introduced in the chapter. Practical exercises are more extensive in the chapters that deal with basic statistics.

The overall purpose of this book is to help develop skills, abilities and competencies, and other educational attributes such as knowledge, comprehension, analysis, application, synthesis and evaluation. *Knowledge* refers mainly to memorising, defining, describing, identifying, recognising and recalling facts, concepts, theories, etc. *Comprehension* implies translating, integrating and extrapolating. *Analysis* relates to identifying, categorising, comparing, discriminating and recognising set elements. *Application* is the ability to use new materials in practical situations: constructing, developing, planning, applying, building and solving. *Synthesis* involves combining and integrating elements with the purpose of creating, developing and explaining, as well as formulating and proposing plans and solutions. *Evaluation* is the ability to make judgements, that is, deciding, appraising, and criticising.

It is hoped that this workbook will help to make reading the accompanying text, *Social Research*, enjoyable and learning social research methods challenging and worthwhile.

Sotirios Sarantakos
August 1997

1

Introduction

Contents

Educational objectives

After completing this chapter, you will:

1   have a good grounding in the historical development and theoretical founda-
    tions of social research;
2   have knowledge of the main elements of positivism and positivist method-
    ology and its impact on modern social research;

3   have an understanding of the changes and development in the area of method-
    ological thinking, following the decrease of the domination of positivism in
    the social sciences;
4   be able to recognise the varieties of social research and their purpose in the
    social sciences;
5   have a critical understanding of the aims and motives of social research;
6   be in a position to appreciate the debate about objectivity in the social sci-
    ences and the significance of this issue for social research;
7   have knowledge of the role of ethics in social research and its significance for
    the individual and the community;
8   be in a position to see social research as a pluralistic enterprise, employing a
    variety of frameworks and aiming at a multiplicity of goals, and not as a
    monolithic tool of social sciences;
9   be in a position to see research in context and in connection with theoretical,
    political and historical developments;
10 have established the historical foundations of social research.

Main points

The main points made in this chapter are:

1   Social research has a long history. It has been used extensively for more than
    2000 years.
2   Social research as we know it today was introduced by Comte in 1848.
3   The theoretical basis of Comte's social research is positivism.
4   Positivistic research is developed with the intention of being 'scientific'.
5   Positivism and positivist research have dominated the research scene for the
    largest part of the history of the social sciences. Positivistic research is still
    the most dominant type of research in the social sciences.
6   Positivistic research was challenged by a number of schools of thought. The
    most serious criticisms came from symbolic interactionism, ethnomethod-
    ology, phenomenology and philosophical hermeneutics.
7   Criticisms came also from Marxists, feminists and supporters of action
    research.
8   Some of the criticisms centred on perception of reality, the methods it used,
    the relationship between researcher and researched, the goals it served and
    the politics of research.
9   There are many types of research. The overarching divisions in social
    research are qualitative and quantitative research.
10 Quantitative and qualitative research have different ways of approaching,
    developing and assessing theories.
11 Quantitative and qualitative research vary in terms of the logic of theory, the
    direction of theory building, verification, concepts and generalisations.
12 The aims of research vary according to the type of underlying methodology.
    Positivists aim to explore, explain, evaluate, predict and to develop/test
    theories; interpretivists to understand human behaviour; and critical theorists
    to criticise social reality, emancipate, empower and liberate people, and pro-
    pose solutions to social problems.

13 The motives of research are educational, 'magical', personal, institutional, political and tactical.
14 The principles of research are precision in measurement, validity, reliability, objectivity, representativenes, replication and ethics.
15 Objectivity excludes personal values from research; it expects research to be value free and to study 'what is' and not 'what ought to be'.
16 Objectivity is a controversial issue and is still being debated in the social sciences. Many consider it unattainable, unnecessary and undesirable.
17 Objectivity has been contested in quantitative and qualitative research and, although it is weaker than before, many researchers still adhere to it.
18 Adherence to ethical standards is expected in quantitative and qualitative research. Ethics relates to professional practice, the researcher–respondent relationship, the researcher–researcher relationship, and the researcher–animal relationship.
19 Representativeness is an important characteristic of social research that is closely adhered to in quantitative research, but to a lesser extent in qualitative research.
20 The politics of research is very strong and must not be underestimated.

Short-answer questions

The best way of assuring that you have fully understood what you have worked through in this chapter is to ask yourself relevant questions. Below are a few examples. It is advisable that you answer each question carefully, turning to your Social Research *text for assistance when your memory fails you or when you are in doubt about the accuracy of your responses. You may write down your answers if you wish, but just reading each question and finding a satisfactory answer is equally helpful.*

1 What is meant by positivism and in which ways did this theory influence social research?
2 What were the main reasons for the shift away from positivism?
3 In what ways are alternative research models different from the positivistic model?
4 What are the main aims of social research?
5 What are the major types of social research?
6 How can research be used/misused in modern societies?
7 In what ways and to what extent has ideology influenced the form, type and outcomes of social research?
8 What are the main principles of quantitative research?
9 What is the essence of the debate about objectivity in social research?
10 Should social scientists be subjective or objective in their research?
11 What do you understand under normativism and how does it perceive social research?
12 To what extent is objectivity possible?
13 To what extent is subjectivity desirable?
14 Are value neutrality and normativism compatible in any way and to any extent in social research?

15   What is the essence of the debate about ethics in social research?
16   In which areas of research is ethics relevant?
17   What are the areas in which research can violate the code of ethics?
18   What is meant by representativeness and what is its significance for social research?
19   What types of generalisations are allowed in quantitative and qualitative research?
20   What are the limitations of social research?
21   How can politics affect research, the choice of research topic and research outcomes?

Definitions of concepts

In this and the following chapters you will be asked to define a number of key concepts, introduced for the first time, or considered important for understanding aspects of the theme of the chapter. Ideally, you should write down a brief definition of these concepts. However, given the size of the task, you may write the 'skeleton' of the definition on the line provided. Make sure your definition is correct. If in doubt, consult your text.

Action research

....

Causal explanation

....

Causal research

....

Ethics

....

Explanatory research

....

Exploratory research

....

Logical positivism

....

Normativism

....

Objectivity

....

Positive phenomena

....

Participatory research

....

Positivism

....

Positivististic methodology

....

Qualitative research

....

Quantitative research

....

Theories

....

Value neutrality

....

Multiple-choice questions

Answers to these multiple-choice questions are given at the end of the chapter.

1   Positivism proposes that
   a   one should enter the research process with a positive attitude
   b   positive phenomena do not exist
   c   research should investigate positive phenomena only
   d   one should avoid negative impressions of reality

2   Positivism was developed and introduced to the social sciences by
   a   Spencer
   b   Plato
   c   Comte
   d   Marx

3   Positivist principles as introduced by Comte entailed an aversion to
    a   speculation
    b   metaphysics
    c   theological explanations
    d   all of the above

4   Positivism suggests that social sciences should
    a   adopt the scientific method
    b   employ the positive method
    c   study positive phenomena
    d   all of the above

5   Symbolic interactionism
    a   helped develop the basic elements of 'positive methods'
    b   is theoretically and methodologically in accord with positivist principles
    c   objected strongly to positivist principles of social research
    d   is the result of positivist efforts to establish a realistic methodology

6   The Frankfurt School adheres to methodological principles that
    a   are in accord with positivist thinking
    b   are different but compatible to positivist principles
    c   are contrary to positivist theory and methodology
    d   are akin to the philosophical principles of positivism of the early 1800s

7   Marxists from the very beginning
    a   supported positivism as long as it favoured the struggles of the oppressed
    b   sharply criticised positivism for a number of reasons
    c   were divided about the relevance of positivism for the class struggle
    d   all of the above

8   Feminists criticised positivist research for
    a   having a gendered character
    b   being based on a male paradigm
    c   for placing women in a position of inferiority
    d   all of the above

9   General criticisms of positivism addressed
    a   its perception of reality
    b   the goals it pursued
    c   the moral prescriptions it assumed
    d   all of the above

10   Qualitative research is one that
    a   is based on theories such as symbolic interactionism and phenomenology
    b   is geared towards exploration of social relationships
    c   describes reality as experienced by researchers
    d   all of the above

11 Which of the following criteria of action research is *not* one of the four proposed by Burns?

    a action is situational

    b action is collaborative

    c action is value free and objective

    d action is participatory

12 Which of the following is *not* one of the conditions that should be met when causation is to be established?

    a a relationship between variables must be established

    b time order must be established

    c teleology must be evident

    d cause and effects must be contiguous

13 Which of the following is *not* one of the problems referred to in the text that may interfere with establishing a causal relationship?

    a mismatch

    b rationale of causation

    c spuriousness

    d tautology

14 Which of the following statements is *not* correct?

    a in qualitative research, theory is deductive; in qualitative research, theory is inductive

    b quantitative research begins with reality, qualitative research begins with theory

    c quantitative research employs fixed concepts, qualitative research employs sensitising concepts

    d quantitative research allows inductive generalisations, qualitative research makes analytic generalisations

15 Which of the following does *not* belong to the aims of positivist research?

    a to emancipate people

    b to explore social reality

    c to explain social phenomena

    d to make predictions

16 Which of the following is *not* one of the principles of social research?

    a spuriousness

    b replication

    c precision in measurement

    d representativeness

17 Value neutrality is the same as

    a normativism

    b objectivity

    c reliability

    d naturalism

18   Value neutrality suggests that
    a   social sciences should study 'what is' and not 'what ought to be'
    b   researchers must be objective
    c   researchers ought to be limited in their personal biases
    d   all of the above

19   Normativism is
    a   the same as objectivism
    b   the same as value neutrality
    c   the opposite of value neutrality
    d   **a** and **b** above

20   Which of the following statements is *not* correct?
    a   normativists suggest that objectivity is unattainable, unnecessary and undesirable
    b   according to normativism social scientists ought to have no views on social issues
    c   normativists argue that our general orientation is based on and guided by values
    d   normativists suggest that disclosing our personal bias is less dangerous than pretending to be value free

21   Feminists argue that
    a   objectivity has adverse effects on women
    b   abandoning objectivity may eliminate constraints that dominate the essence of women
    c   feminist research must be based on objectivity if women are to be liberated
    d   **a** and **b** are correct

22   In qualitative research, objectivity
    a   is rejected
    b   is accepted under certain conditions
    c   is accepted in certain types of studies
    d   **b** and **c** are correct

23   Which of the following reasons against objectivity is *not* one of those proposed by qualitative researchers?
    a   objectivity implies distance and neutrality from the researched
    b   objectivity is desirable during research design but not during data analysis
    c   objectivity implies that reality is objectively given
    d   objectivity emerges out of subjectivity

24   Which of the following is one of the ethical standards in professional practice?
    a   accuracy in data gathering, data processing, and reporting
    b   choice of relevant research methodology and use of appropriate interpretation
    c   avoiding fabrication or falsification of data
    d   all of the above

25 Theoretical sampling is one that
   a is based on sampling theory
   b results in refining sampling theory
   c is geared towards theoretically important units
   d is none of the above

Answers to multiple-choice questions

1 c	**6** c	**11** c	**16** a	**21** d
2 c	**7** b	**12** c	**17** b	**22** a
3 d	**8** d	**13** b	**18** d	**23** b
4 d	**9** d	**14** b	**19** c	**24** d
5 c	**10** d	**15** a	**20** b	**25** c

2

Varieties of social research

Contents

   c Feminist research and conventional research
   d Is there a feminist methodology?
13 Summary

Educational objectives

After completing this chapter, you will:

1 have a clear idea of the distinction between perspectives, paradigms, methods and methodologies;
2 understand the main elements of the main paradigms employed in the social sciences;
3 have knowledge of the theoretical perspectives explained in this unit and the differences between them;
4 be aware of the detailed differences between the various perspectives on specific theoretical criteria;
5 have a thorough understanding of the differences between quantitative and qualitative methodologies;
6 be in a position to appreciate the value of the two methodologies and be aware of their advantages and disadvantages;
7 have knowledge of feminist methods and their relation to the various methodologies;
8 have a critical understanding of feminist research and how it differs from other research methods;
9 have developed the skills that are required to choose the right methodology;
10 have developed a balanced view of methodologies currently used by researchers in the social sciences.

Main points

The main points made in this chapter are:

1 It is important to distinguish between perspectives, paradigms, methodologies and methods.
2 A perspective is the standpoint researchers use to study the world. It is often taken to be synonymous with a paradigm.
3 A paradigm is a set of propositions that explains how the world is perceived.
4 A methodology is a model entailing the theoretical principles and frameworks that provide the guidelines that show how research is to be done.
5 A method is a tool or an instrument employed by researchers to collect data.
6 The main methodological perspectives in the social sciences are the positivistic, the interpretive and the critical perspectives.
7 Examples of paradigms developed within the positivist perspective are positivism, neopositivism and logical positivism.

8   Examples of paradigms developed within the interpretive perspective are symbolic interactionism, phenomenology, ethnomethodology, hermeneutics, psychoanalysis, ethnology, ethnography and sociolinguistics.

9   Examples of paradigms developed within the critical perspective are critical sociology, conflict school of thought, Marxism and feminism.

10 Methodologies vary fundamentally from each other. However, they can use the same or similar methods.

11 The three methodological perspectives vary from each other in terms of how they perceive reality, human beings, science, and research.

12 Quantitative methodology takes a strict, objective, neutral and 'scientific' stance and employs a perspective which resembles that of the natural sciences.

13 Quantitative methodology has been criticised, among other things, for the way in which it perceives reality, people and research, the methods it uses, the politics it supports and the relationship it establishes with the researched.

14 Qualitative methodology adopts a subjective perception of reality and employs a naturalistic type of inquiry. Its central principles are openness, process-nature of the research and the object, reflexivity of object and analysis, explication and flexibility.

15 Qualitative methodology has been criticised, among other things, for not being able to cope with demands related to reliability, representativeness, generalisability, objectivity and detachment, ethics and the value of collected data.

16 Quantitative methodology sees reality as objective and simple, qualitative methodology as subjective and problematic.

17 Quantitative methodology explains human action in terms of nomological principles, qualitative methodology explains human action in non-deterministic terms.

18 Quantitative methodology supports a value-free inquiry, qualitative methodology a value-bound inquiry.

19 Quantitative methodology is deductive, qualitative methodology is inductive.

20 The researcher is rather passive and the 'knower' in quantitative research, but active and interactive in qualitative research.

21 Qualitative research entails subject-directed paradigms, object-directed paradigms and development-directed paradigms.

22 Quantitative and qualitative methodology are equally valuable and useful in their own context.

23 Feminist research is most useful and very popular. It has a place in social research.

24 Feminist research employs mostly qualitative methods and to a lesser extent quantitative methods. The methods that can be characterised as exclusively 'feminist' are rare.

25 Characteristic for feminist research is not the methods it employs but its epistemology.

26 Feminist research has not yet developed the parameters that are required for the development of a 'methodology'.

Short-answer questions

The first step to learning is to establish basic knowledge and comprehension of the material you read. Beyond this, you are expected to develop the skills that are required to apply, analyse, synthesise and evaluate material. The questions listed below are designed to help you test the level to which you have succeeded in your study and to identify gaps. As in the previous chapter, check with your Social Research *text to see whether you have formed the right impression of the issues discussed in this chapter.*

1   Name the three most important sociological perspectives that influenced the nature and process of social research. Describe their major differences.
2   What are the main assumptions of qualitative methodology?
3   What is the meaning of the thesis of 'nomological thinking'?
4   List five major 'problems' of quantitative methodology.
5   What do critics mean when they say that positivistic research fails to distinguish between appearance and reality?
6   Quantitative methodology is criticised for being technocratic. What does this mean and why is it considered a problem?
7   What are the general criteria of qualitative methodology?
8   From which theories does qualitative methodology draw its major theoretical guidelines and principles?
9   What is meant by naturalistic method and what is its significance for social research?
10   What are the central principles of qualitative research? Describe and evaluate their significance for social research.
11   What is meant by 'openness' in qualitative research?
12   What are the research foundations of qualitative research?
13   Define in your own words the concept 'reflective research'.
14   Describe five important differences between quantitative and qualitative research.
15   In what ways is feminist research different from quantitative research?
16   In what ways is feminist research different from qualitative research?
17   What are the arguments in favour of and against feminist methodology?
18   Which type of research is most effective: quantitative, qualitative or feminist research?

Definitions of concepts

Define the following concepts:

Androcentricity

....

Critical perspective

....

Explication

....

Flexibility

....

Feminist methods

....

Gender insensitivity

....

Gynopia

....

Hermeneutics

....

Interpretive paradigm

....

Method

....

Methodology

....

Misogyny

....

Openness

....

Paradigms

....

Phenomenology

....

Reflexivity

....

Sexual dichotomism

....

Symbolic interactionism

....

Multiple-choice questions

Answers to these multiple-choice questions are given at the end of the chapter.

1   A set of propositions that explain how the world is perceived is
    a   a methodology
    b   a paradigm
    c   method
    d   all of the above

2   A model that entails theoretical principles as well as a framework for social research is
    a   a methodology
    b   a paradigm
    c   method
    d   all of the above

3   Which of the following theoretical perspectives stresses *verstehen*, that is, sympathetic understanding as its goal?
    a   positivism
    b   interpretivism
    c   critical perspective
    d   conflict theory

4   Which theory of those listed below sees reality as everything perceived through the senses?
    a   positivist perspective
    b   interpretivist perspective
    c   critical perspective
    d   conflict perspective

5   Which theoretical perspective perceives human beings as rational individuals governed by social laws?
    a   positivist perspective
    b   interpretive perspective
    c   critical perspective
    d   both **b** and **c**

6   Which of the theoretical perspectives listed below distinguish between appearance and reality?
a positivism
b interpretivism
c critical perspective
d both **a** and **b**

7   Which of the theories listed below perceive reality as being dominated by conflicts and tensions?
a positivism
b Marxism
c feminism
d both **b** and **c**

8   The notion that science is based on strict procedures and not on common sense is proposed by
a the positivists
b the interactionists
c the interpretivists
d the critical theorists

9   The notion that science is nomothetic means that
a science has the purpose of helping introduce laws (*nomos* = law)
b science is based on universal laws
c research has the purpose of discovering laws where others cannot see them
d none of the above

10   The notion that knowledge is derived through the senses only is held by
a positivism
b symbolic interactionism
c interpretivism
d critical perspective

11   The notion that science is inductive, proceeding from the specific to the general and from the concrete to the abstract is held by
a positivism
b interpretive perspective
c critical theory
d both **a** and **b**

12   Which of the theories listed below proposes that the purpose of research is to understand people?
a positivism
b interpretive perspective
c critical perspective
d **a** and **b** above

13 The notion that explanation is derived exclusively from experience is proposed by
   a positivism
   b symbolic interactionism
   c interpretive perspective
   d critical perspective

14 The notion that facts should be kept apart from values is proposed by
   a positivism
   b symbolic interactionism
   c interpretive perspective
   d critical perspective

15 The view that the social world is a human creation not a discovery is proposed by
   a positivism
   b neopositivism
   c interpretive perspective
   d critical perspective

16 Which of the following is *not* one of the six central principles of qualitative methodology?
   a openness
   b retrospectivity
   c reflexivity
   d flexibility

17 Which of the following is *not* one of the strengths of qualitative research?
   a qualitative research offers a more realistic view of the world
   b qualitative research offers deep understanding of the respondents' world
   c qualitative research offers quick data collection
   d qualitative research offers high flexibility

18 The concept 'gynopia' is used to describe the situation where
   a women cannot see faults of the system due to conditioning
   b women are invisible in society
   c the world is seen through the eyes of women
   d both **a** and **b**

Practical exercises

1 Choose two articles from professional journals. The articles should be chosen so that the one employs a quantitative and the other a qualitative methodology.

2 Describe in point form the attributes that make the articles 'quantitative' and 'qualitative'.

3   Contrast the two articles in terms of their background methodologies so that their nature becomes clear and obvious.

4   Show which of the two articles was more successful in answering the research questions.

5   Discuss critically the social significance of these articles, that is, the extent to which they contributed to gaining knowledge about the issue they investigated.

Answers to multiple-choice questions

1 b	**5** a	**9** b	**13** a	**17** c
2 a	**6** c	**10** a	**14** a	**18** b
3 b	**7** d	**11** b	**15** c	
4 a	**8** a	**12** b	**16** b	

3

Measurement and scaling

Contents

Educational objectives

After completing this chapter, you will:

1 have a good understanding of how and why measurement is used in social research;
2 have a clear understanding of the purpose and usefulness of measurement;
3 have knowledge of the logical basis of the factors that guide measurement;
4 have knowledge of the extent to which measurement is employed in quantitative and qualitative research;
5 be able to distinguish between the various levels of measurement and their purpose in social research;
6 have a critical understanding of validity and reliability in social research;
7 be in a position to employ the various scaling techniques described in this chapter;
8 be able to develop scales in the context of a project in which you may be involved;
9 be a critical reader of reports containing measurement, validity, reliability and scaling;
10 be aware of the theoretical and methodological principles of the various schools of thought relating to measurement, scaling, validity and reliability.

Main points

The main points made in this chapter are:

1 Some form and degree of measurement is included in all types of research.
2 A variable is a concept that can take two or more values.
3 Variables can be discrete or continuous; they vary in terms of scale continuity.
4 There are four levels of measurement: nominal, ordinal, interval and ratio levels.
5 Nominal level measurement involves classification of events to categories.
6 Ordinal-level measurement involves categorising, ordering and ranking according to magnitude.
7 Interval level measurement displays the values of nominal and ordinal-level measurement but it also contains equal intervals.
8 Ratio level measurement is an interval ratio measurement but it also contains an absolute true zero.
9 Variables are measured at the highest level possible
10 Validity is the ability to produce accurate results and to measure what is supposed to be measured.
11 Quantitative research employs many types of validation, for example, empirical, theoretical, face, content and construct validity.
12 Validity is an attribute of quantitative and qualitative research,
13 In qualitative research validation takes the form of cumulative, communicative, argumentative or ecological validation.
14 Reliability is the ability to produce consistent results. Therefore, reliability means consistency.

15 In quantitative research investigators consider many forms of reliability, for example, external or internal reliability and representative or equivalence reliability.

16 In quantitative research, reliability is tested by means of methods such as test-retest method, split-half method, alternate form reliability, etc.

17 Qualitative research aims at assuring reliability but it achieves it by using methods that are different from these employed in quantitative research.

18 An index is a measure containing a combination of items, the values of which are summed up in a numerical score.

19 Scales are used because they offer high coverage, high precision, high reliability, high comparability and simplicity.

20 Examples of such scales are the Thurstone scale, the Likert scale, the Bogardus scale, the Guttman scale, and the semantic differential scale.

Short-answer questions

Answer each question carefully. Consult your Social Research *text when your memory fails you or when you are in doubt about the accuracy of your responses.*

1   Explain the meaning and purpose of measurement the way you understand it.
2   What is the difference between 'common-sense' measurement and methodological measurement?
3   What does qualitative measurement entail?
4   What does quantitative measurement entail?
5   What are the four levels of measurement?
6   What are the main criteria of each of the types of measurement?
7   What are the mathematical principles of each of the four types of measurement?
8   Define in simple terms the nature and principles of validity
9   What is empirical validation?
10 Explain the meaning of concurrent validity.
11 Describe the nature and process of theoretical validation.
12 Explain the nature of face validity.
13 Explain the differences and similarities between content and construct validity.
14 What is the general response of qualitative researchers to validity?
15 Describe the types of validation employed in qualitative research.
16 Which methodology provides a higher level of validity?
17 What is reliability, and how relevant and important is it for social research?
18 What are three types of reliability that are employed in the social sciences?
19 Explain briefly the nature and process of establishing stability reliability, representative reliability and equivalence reliability.
20 Discuss critically the methods employed by social researchers to test reliability.
21 What is the position of qualitative researchers on the notion of reliability?
22 What is the relationship between validity and reliability in social research?
23 What are indexes and how are they employed in social sciences?
24 What are scales and where and how are they employed in social research?

25 What are the basic principles of scale construction?
26 What are the reasons for using scales in social research?
27 Describe the nature and use of Thurstone scales?
28 Describe the nature and usefulness of Likert scales.
29 Describe briefly the steps of construction of Likert scales.
30 Discuss briefly the nature and usefulness of Bogardus social distance scales?
31 What are the purpose and uses of Guttman scales?
32 Describe the steps of construction of Guttman scales.
33 What are 'semantic differential scales' and how are they used in social research?

Definitions of concepts

Define the following concepts:

Alternate-form reliability

....

Argumentative validation

....

Bogardus social distance scale

....

Communicative validation

....

Conceptual frameworks

....

Conceptual validation

....

Concurrent validity

....

Construct validity

....

Content validity

....

Criterion validity

....

Cumulative validation

....

Dependent variable

....

Ecological validation

....

Empirical validation

....

Equivalence reliability

....

External validity

....

Face validity

....

Guttman scale

....

Independent variable

....

Indexes

....

Internal validity

....

Interval level

....

Likert scale

....

Measurement

....

Nominal level measurement

....

Ordinal level measurement

....

Pragmatic validity

....

Qualitative measurement

....

Ratio level measurement

....

Reliability

....

Representative reliability

....

Research model

....

Scaling

....

Semantic differential

....

Split-half method

....

Stability reliability

....

Test-retest method

....

Theoretical validation

....

Thurstone scale

....

Triangulation

....

Unweighted indexes

....

Validity

....

Variable

....

Weighted indexes

....

Multiple-choice questions

Answers to these multiple-choice questions are given at the end of the chapter.

1   A variable
    a   is a concept that can take one or more values
    b   can be 'dependent' in one context and 'independent' in another
    c   is independent if it causes changes to another variable
    d   is all of the above

2   The variables: ethnicity, race, gender, blood type and marital status are
    a   continuous variables
    b   discrete variables
    c   quantitative variables
    d   all of the above

3   Nominal-level measurement shows
    a   the highest and ratio-level measurement, the lowest matching with the real-number system
    b   the lowest and ratio level measurement, the highest matching with the real-number system
    c   the same matching with the real-number system as ratio-level measurement
    d   none of the above

4 Nominal-level measurement
   a is the simplest, lowest and most primitive type of measurement
   b involves classification of events and categories
   c entails 'naming' scales
   d is all of the above

5 In nominal-level measurement
   a categories are distinct, unidimensional, mutually exclusive and exhaustive
   b categories have no mathematical value
   c cannot be added, subtracted, multiplied, divided or otherwise manipulated mathematically
   d all of the above are true

6 Which of the following is *not* correct?
   a nominal measurement has a zero point
   b nominal measurement assumes no equal units of measurement
   c nominal measurement produces nominal or categorical data
   d all of the above

7 Which of the following is correct?
   a ordinal measurement includes categorical variables
   b ordinal measurement is quantitative measurement
   c ordinal measurement fails to offer a relative order of magnitude
   d ordinal measurement shows the amount of difference between the groups

8 Which of the following is correct?
   a interval-level measurement contains equal intervals
   b interval-level measurement is a quantitative measurement
   c interval-level measurement has no true zero point
   d all of the above

9 Which of the following is *not* a characteristic of interval-level measurement?
   a numbers assigned to the categories are used to count and rank
   b numbers assigned to the categories are used to add and subtract
   c numbers assigned to the categories can be multiplied and divided
   d **a** and **b** above

10 Calendar time, degrees of temperature, and IQ scores are examples of
   a nominal-level measurement
   b ordinal-level measurement
   c interval-level measurement
   d ratio-level measurement

11 According to the text, which of the following is *not* correct?
   a ratio-level measurement allows statements about proportions and ratios
   b ratio-level measurement allows the use of all mathematical functions
   c ratio-level measurement is appropriate for attitude measurement
   d all of the above

12 Which of the following is correct with regard to validity?
   a validity is the ability to produce reliable information
   b validity is an attribute of quantitative research only
   c checking for representativeness is a way of validity testing in qualitative research
   d qualitative research uses empirical validation to check validity

13 Which of the following is not one of the tactics of validation used in qualitative research?
   a ruling out spurious relations
   b triangulation
   c pragmatic or criterion validity
   d replicating a finding

14 According to Lamnek, qualitative studies have a higher validity than quantitative studies because
   a the data is closer to reality than in quantitative research
   b a successive expansion of data is possible
   c it allows openness and flexibility in research
   d all of the above

15 According to the text, which of the following types of reliability is *not* considered by quantitative social researchers?
   a stability reliability
   b representative reliability
   c argumentative reliability
   d equivalence reliability

16 Which of the following is *not* one of the methods employed to test reliability in quantitative research?
   a test-retest method
   b increased variability method
   c alternate-form reliability
   d split-half method

17 A method that after four attempts produces the same but incorrect weight of the same person is
   a valid but unreliable
   b reliable but invalid
   c both valid and reliable
   d neither valid nor reliable

18 The time of the day is a
   a continuous variable
   b discrete variable

19 The number of male students in the university bus is a
   a continuous variable
   b discrete variable

20 The percentage of male students in the university tennis club is a
  a continuous variable
  b discrete variable

21 The number of books carried by distinction students to the class is a
  a continuous variable
  b discrete variable

22 The speed at which low performance students complete the exams is a
  a continuous variable
  b discrete variable

23 The weight of students who complete the exams first is a
  a continuous variable
  b discrete variable

24 The age of students who get the most HDs in social research is a
  a continuous variable
  b discrete variable

25 The IQ of female students is an example of a
  a nominal-level measurement
  b ordinal-level measurement
  c interval-level measurement
  d ratio-level measurement

26 The assessment method in social research that extends from poor to good, very good and excellent is an example of
  a nominal-level measurement
  b ordinal-level measurement
  c interval-level measurement
  d ratio-level measurement

27 The types of cars driven by mature-age students are examples of
  a nominal-level measurement
  b ordinal-level measurement
  c interval-level measurement
  d ratio-level measurement

28 The weight of students doing nursing is an example of
  a nominal-level measurement
  b ordinal-level measurement
  c interval-level measurement
  d ratio-level measurement

29 The time required by below average students to complete the end-of-semester examination is an example of
  a nominal-level measurement
  b ordinal-level measurement

c interval-level measurement
d ratio-level measurement

30 According to the text, which of the following factors is one of the reasons for using scales?
a high coverage
b high precision and reliability
c simplicity and high comparability
d all of the above

31 The scale that measures the social distance between certain groups of people is
a the Likert scale
b the Thurstone scale
c the Bogardus scale
d the Guttman scale

Practical exercises

1 Read a journal article that employs quantitative research methods and presents the findings of the study. Try to answer the following questions:
a What type of measurement is employed in this article?
b Is any scale employed in the study?
c Could the investigator have employed other types of measurement or scales in this study?
d Has there been any test of reliability? If yes, which one?
f Has the study employed (implicitly or explicitly) a research model?

2 Find a journal article that employs a qualitative framework. How has the author addressed the research topic? Has there been any form of measurement employed? Have there been any measures taken to deal with validity and reliability?

Answers to multiple-choice questions

1 d	8 d	15 c	22 a	29 d
2 b	9 c	16 b	23 a	30 d
3 b	10 c	17 b	24 a	31 c
4 d	11 c	18 a	25 c	
5 d	12 c	19 b	26 b	
6 a	13 c	20 a	27 a	
7 b	14 d	21 b	28 d	

4

The research process

Contents

Educational objectives

After completing this chapter, you will:

1   have knowledge and a critical understanding of the structure and elements of the research process;
2   be able to distinguish between the steps of the research process in quantitative and qualitative research;
3   have an understanding of the necessity of planning in research as a systematic exploration of reality and as a tool of acquisition of knowledge;
4   have knowledge of how evaluation research is conducted and how different it is from the standard research process;
5   have an understanding of the process, aims and main characteristics of action research and its place in the social sciences.

Main points

The main points made in this chapter are:

1 The research process is often presented in the form of a model.
2 Research is assumed to progress in a set of steps that are executed in a prescribed order.
3 The use of a research model guides research planning and action and brings many advantages to the research project.
4 The steps of a research model are preparation, research design, data collection, data processing and reporting.
5 Research preparation entails selection of methodology, selection and definition of the research topic, exploration, operationalisation and formulation of hypotheses.
6 Research designs refer to the selection of the sample and to the methods of data collection and analysis, as well as to arrangements of administrative procedures.
7 Data collection entails decisions and action regarding the collection of the information required to address the research question.
8 Data processing entails grouping, presentation, analysis and interpretation of the findings.
9 Reporting refers to the process of publication of the findings.
10 Qualitative research does not adhere strictly to the rules described above. Nevertheless, some form of a model is employed in this type of research.
11 Some writers on qualitative research speak of conceptual frameworks rather than research models.
12 Evaluation research has the purpose of assessing the quality, effectiveness and suitability of program plans and programs.
13 There are many types of evaluation research, for example, feasibility studies, process analysis and impact analysis.
14 The overall design of evaluation research resembles that of the standard research model described in this chapter.
15 Action research is defined as 'the application of fact finding to practical problem solving in a social situation with a view to improving the quality of action within it, involving the collaboration and cooperation of researchers, practitioners and laymen'.
16 Action research differs from the mainstream type of research in the extent to which researchers and subjects are involved in the research process and in the political nature of the research.

Short-answer questions

Answer each question carefully. Consult your Social Research *text when your memory fails you or when you are in doubt about the accuracy of your responses.*

1 What are the basic assumptions about social research as a process?
2 What is the purpose of a research model?

3   List five major decisions that are usually made during the planning of a research model.
4   What are the major steps of the research model?
5   Why is it necessary that a decision is made early in the study about the research methodology to be employed in the project?
6   How different are the research models employed by qualitative and quantitative researchers?
7   List three major differences between the research models employed by quantitative and qualitative researchers
8   What is meant by conceptual frameworks and research models?
9   What are the main goals of evaluation research?
10 How different from other research models is the research model that is employed in evaluation research?
11 What are the main criteria of action research?
12 Does action research comply with the objectivity requirements that are required in social research?
13 How valid are the findings produced by means of action research?
14 How different is the research model applied by action researchers from that of other investigators?

Definitions of concepts

Define the following concepts:

Action research

....

Bounding

....

Conceptual frameworks

....

Design

....

Evaluation research

....

Execution

....

Feasibility study

....

Focusing

....

Impact analysis

....

Process analysis

....

Processing

....

Reporting

....

Research model

....

Research preparation

....

Research steps

....

Multiple-choice questions

Answers to these multiple choice questions are given at the end of the chapter.

1   According to the text, which of the following assumptions made by researchers who employ a research model is correct?
   a research can be perceived as evolving in a sequence of steps, the success of which depends upon successful completion of the previous step
   b steps must be executed in the given order
   c research is more successful if it is guided by a research model
   d all of the above

2   Which of the following statements is correct?
   a in all research models the decision about sampling comes first because of its significance for the research outcomes
   b in all research models decisions about research methodology are excluded from the research model because they may bias the researcher
   c in all research models, progression from sampling to data collection and data analysis is a must and takes place without exception
   d none of the above

3   Which of the following does *not* belong to the goals of a research model?
    a it offers guidance and direction to research, helping reduce time and costs
    b it introduces a systematic approach to social investigation, encouraging effectiveness and economy in procedure
    c it introduces an effective organisation, coordination and management of the project
    d none of the above

4   Qualitative studies
    a use no designs of research models
    b are incompatible with research designs and models
    c use research models and designs adopted to their needs and theoretical principles
    d use the same designs and models as quantitative studies

5   The research model employed in evaluation research and action research
    a is fundamentally different from that employed in other types of research
    b is different from that employed in other types of research
    c shares some of the steps of the research model employed in other types of research but is still different
    d is fairly similar to that employed in other types of research

Practical exercises

1   Assume you are researching husband abuse in Darwin. You have adequate resources to investigate this family issue and you are ready to begin the project.
    a Show the steps of your research design, if you were to employ a quantitative methodology.
    b Show the steps of your research design, if you were to employ a qualitative methodology.
    c Explain the major theoretical and methodological differences between these two models and their advantages and disadvantages.

2   Following the path described in the previous example, construct a research model to be employed in the study of same-sex couples in a small country town.

It goes without saying that you are not yet expected to have the knowledge and skills required for developing a full-scale research model with all details regarding sampling procedures and methods of data collection. These issues will be discussed later. At this stage, you are expected to describe the steps of the research process, to demonstrate the interconnections of the various steps involved in it and to concentrate mainly on the overall picture rather than on the specific details.

Answers to multiple-choice questions

1 d   2 d   3 d   4 c   5 d

5

Initiating social research

Contents

Educational objectives

After completing this chapter, you will:

1 have knowledge of how research topics are selected and prepared for research;
2 be aware of the process of theoretical formulation of the research topic;
3 have an understanding of the process of operationalisation and its workings and usefulness for social research;
4 be able to prepare an exploratory study and justify its place in social research;
5 have a thorough understanding of the structure and purpose of hypotheses and be able to justify their place in quantitative and qualitative research;
6 be in a position to complete the first stage of social research and place it logically and methodologically in the context of a research project;
7 be in a position to distinguish between the tasks involved in preparing social research in a quantitative and a qualitative context;
8 have a critical understanding of the purpose of the steps of research preparation for the research project and social research in general.

Main points

The main points made in this chapter are:

1 Research initiation entails the selection of methodology, the selection and definition of the research topic, the decision to conduct an exploratory study, operationalisation and formulation of hypotheses.
2 The research topic is usually chosen by the researcher but it can also be determined by social circumstances or the sponsor.
3 Most issues are researchable.
4 The choice of methodology varies with a number of factors, of which the personal choice of the researcher and the nature of the topic are two.
5 Defining the research topic before the research has begun is a common practice and also imperative for quantitative social researchers but not for qualitative researchers.
6 Exploratory studies involve review of literature, expert surveys and analysis of case studies.
7 The goals of exploratory studies are to establish feasibility of the study, to familiarise the researcher with the research topic and the respondents, to bring new ideas to the research, and to facilitate operationalisation and the formulation of hypotheses.
8 Operationalisation is the process of quantifying variables for the purpose of measuring their occurrence, strength and frequency.
9 The process of operationalisation entails selection and quantification of indicators, and quantification of the variable.
10 The rules of operationalisation are the rule of empirical relevance, the rule of correspondence, the rule of empirical adequacy and the rule of quantification.
11 Qualitative researchers do not use operationalisation; instead they use 'sensitising concepts'.

12 A hypothesis is an assumption about the status of events or about relations between variables.

13 Hypotheses are expected to adhere to certain rules, for example, to be clear, specific, precise and empirically testable; must describe one issue at a time; and must not contain statements that are contradictory.

14 There are many types of hypotheses, for example, working hypotheses, statistical hypotheses, research hypotheses, null hypotheses, alternative hypotheses and scientific hypotheses.

15 Qualitative researchers accept the use of hypotheses but employ them in a different manner and in a different context.

Short-answer questions

Answer each question carefully. Consult your Social Research *text when your memory fails you or when you are in doubt about the accuracy of your responses.*

1 What are the factors that can limit the choice of topics in social research?

2 How can social reality influence the choice of a research question?

3 In what ways can contract research influence the choice of the research topic and the quality of social research in general?

4 What are the implications of persons other than the researcher controlling the choice of research topics for social research in general and for academics in particular?

5 What is the purpose of the step 'preparation'?

6 What does a formal definition of the topic entail?

7 What is meant by 'exploration' in social research?

8 How important is the step 'defining variables' for quantitative and qualitative researchers?

9 How relevant for qualitative research are exploratory studies as described in this chapter?

10 What are the types of exploratory research?

11 Discuss briefly the purpose and structure of the types of exploratory studies.

12 Give a brief definition and description of operationalisation.

13 What does the process of operationalisation entail?

14 Define the essence and purpose of indicators in social research.

15 What are the general rules that guide operationalisation?

16 Explain the rule of empirical relevance.

17 What is meant by the rule of empirical adequacy?

18 What does the rule of quantification involve and what is its purpose?

19 Explain how indicators are selected.

20 Do qualitative researchers employ operationalisation?

21 What are the main objections qualitative researchers have to operationalisation?

22 Why is operationalisation considered by qualitative researchers as inadequate, incomplete and subjective?

23 What is a hypothesis?

24 What are the criteria of hypothesis construction?

25 In what ways can hypotheses be generated?

26   Are hypotheses required in social research? Are they useful? Why?

27   What are the major types of hypotheses?

28   What are working hypotheses and where are they mainly used?

29   What are the functions of hypotheses?

30   In what ways can the use of hypotheses limit the process and effects of social research?

31   If you were a qualitative researcher, how would you criticise the use of hypotheses?

32   If you were a quantitative researcher how would you defend the use of hypotheses in social research?

Definitions of concepts

Define the following concepts:

Alternative hypotheses

....

Case studies

....

Empirical adequacy

....

Empirical relevance

....

Expert surveys

....

Exploration

....

Hypotheses

....

Indicators

....

Literature review

....

Null hypotheses

....

Operationalisation

....

Research hypotheses

....

Scientific hypotheses

....

Statistical hypotheses

....

Working hypotheses

....

Multiple-choice questions

Answers to these multiple-choice questions are given at the end of the chapter.

1 Which of the following is *not* correct?
    a qualitative studies use no operationalisation
    b sampling in qualitative studies is representative
    c qualitative studies allow inductive not analytical generalisations
    d qualitative studies employ designs that are loosely structured

2 The concept analytical generalisations means that
    a generalisations are based on accurate statistical analysis of data
    b generalisations are subject, context and time specific
    c generalisations are derived from secondary analysis of data
    d both **a** and **b** are correct

3 Qualitative studies
    a use no hypotheses in their operation
    b develop hypotheses during the first step of the research process and prove or disprove them during the study
    c develop hypotheses at the end of the study
    d none of the above statements is correct

4 Miles and Huberman are reported in the text as suggesting that conceptual frameworks
    a are simply the current version of the researcher's map of the territory being investigated
    b are not blinkers or straitjackets but emerge and are revised and adjusted during the research
    c are important and without them research becomes a fruitless research anarchy
    d demonstrate all the criteria listed above

5   Which of the following factors is *not* one of those reported by Berger as influencing the choice of a research methodology?
    a   the appropriateness of the method for the theoretical goals
    b   the adequacy of the method for the research object
    c   the ideological orientation of the researcher (for example, feminist, Marxist, structuralist)
    d   prerequisites and conditions of research

6   Which of the following does *not* belong to the process of formulating the research question?
    a   definition of the topic
    b   sampling
    c   exploration
    d   operationalisation

7   Which of the following is one of the reasons for undertaking exploration?
    a   to test feasibility of the study
    b   to familiarise the researcher with the context of the issue in question
    c   to assist with the formulation of hypothesis
    d   all of the above

8   Which of the following is *not* one of the types of exploratory studies?
    a   review of literature
    b   pre-tests and pilot studies
    c   expert surveys
    d   analysis of case studies

9   Which of the following is *not* one of the rules of operationalisation referred to in the text?
    a   the rule of selectivity
    b   the rule of empirical relevance
    c   the rule of empirical adequacy
    d   the rule of quantification

10 Which of the following are *not* one of the criticisms qualitative researchers have of operationalisation?
    a   operationalisation often does not link concepts with reality but concepts with other concepts
    b   operationalisation is completed after the research has begun and is therefore irrelevant
    c   operationalisation cannot possibly cover all aspects of the concept
    d   operationalisation is subjective: it relies very much on the personal views of the researcher

11 Which of the following is *not* one of the criteria of hypothesis construction referred to in the text?
    a   hypotheses must predict accurately the outcome of the study
    b   hypotheses must contain statements that are not contradictory
    c   hypotheses must describe variables or relationships between variables
    d   hypotheses must describe one variable at a time

12 Which of the following is one of the functions of hypotheses mentioned in the text?
   a to guide social research
   b to enable the researcher to concentrate on an issue of particular importance
   c to facilitate statistical analysis in the context of hypothesis testing
   d all of the above

Practical exercises

1 Assume that you were to study 'feminism' in a country town. Explain briefly:
   a how you would approach this issue conceptually;
   b how you would 'measure' feminism, if you employed a quantitative methodology?
   c how you would address feminism, if you employed a qualitative methodology?

2 Formulate three hypotheses to be employed in a quantitative study of the relationship between television viewing and the incidence of rape.

Answers to multiple-choice questions

1 c	**4** d	**7** d	**10** b
2 b	**5** c	**8** b	**11** a
3 c	**6** b	**9** a	**12** d

6

Sampling procedures

Contents

Educational objectives

After completing this chapter, you will:

1   be able to explain the nature and process of sampling in social research;
2   understand the main types of sampling and the areas in which they can be applied;
3   have knowledge of the advantages and disadvantages of sampling in general and of the sampling methods in particular;
4   be in a position to apply sampling in actual situations;
5   have a clear understanding of the ways in which sampling procedures are employed in qualitative and quantitative research, and their logical and methodological foundation.

Main points

The main points made in this chapter are:

1   Sampling is the process of choosing the respondents and the units of the study in general.
2   Sampling is a common practice and an indispensable research tool in social sciences.
3   Sampling, as the alternative to conducting a saturation survey, offers many advantages.
4   Sampling units must be chosen objectively and systematically, must be easily identifiable and clearly defined, independent from each other, not inter-changeable, and free of errors, bias and distortions.
5   The two distinct types of sampling are probability and non-probability sampling.
6   In a probability sampling, all units have an equal, calculable and non-zero probability to be included in the sample.
7   Non-probability sampling does not adhere to the rules of probability.
8   The two types of probability sampling are simple random sampling and systematic sampling.
9   In a simple random sampling all units of the target population have an equal chance of being selected.
10   The three most common techniques of selection used in simple random sampling are the lottery method, the method of random numbers and the computer method.
11   In systematic sampling although all units have an equal chance of being selected, their selection depends on the choice of other units.
12   Systematic sampling employs the sampling fraction method of choosing the respondents.
13   Stratified random sampling is the procedure in which the sample is chosen after the target population is divided in a number of strata, from which the respondents are taken.
14   Cluster sampling is the procedure in which in the first instance clusters are chosen.

15   In multi-stage sampling, samples are chosen in stages: firstly one sample is taken and then a second or third sample is chosen from within the previous sample.

16   In multi-phase sampling the procedure followed is the same as in multi-stage sampling with the difference that in each stage of sampling data is collected.

17   Area sampling is the procedure in which the choice of respondents is related to geographical areas. An area is divided into smaller sections, progressively leading to smaller samples and ultimately to the respondents.

18   Panel samples include a number of respondents chosen in a systematic way and subjected to data collection on more than one occasion.

20   Spatial sampling is a procedure in which a sample is taken from people temporarily congregated in space.

21   Accidental sampling is a non-probability sampling procedure in which the researcher chooses a number of respondents at will. It is also called convenience sampling, chunk sampling, grab sampling or haphazard sampling.

22   In purposive sampling the researcher chooses the respondents who are thought to serve the purpose of the study. It is also called judgemental sampling.

23   Quota sampling is the procedure in which the researcher chooses a quota of respondents set by the project manager

24   Snowball sampling is a procedure in which the selection of additional respondents is guided by respondents who have already been studied.

25   In theoretical sampling the choice of respondents is guided by the emerging theory.

26   Sampling procedures are employed in all quantitative studies but elements of sampling are found also in qualitative research.

27   Non-response is a serious research problem that investigators must deal with.

28   Sample size is determined in statistical and non-statistical terms.

Short-answer questions

Answer each question carefully. Consult your Social Research *text when your memory fails you or when you are in doubt about the accuracy of your responses.*

1   Give a brief description of the nature and purpose of sampling in quantitative and qualitative research.

2   What is a complete coverage study?

3   What is meant by a 'saturation survey'?

4   Describe briefly the differences between target population and survey population.

5   List the main reasons for employing sampling procedures.

6   In what ways can a study based on sampling offer more detailed information than a saturation study?

7   Discuss briefly the main principles of sampling.

8   What are the basic types of sampling? List their main similarities and differences.

9   What are the most common types of probability sampling?

10   Describe the method of random numbers in sampling.

11 How are samples established when using the lottery method of selection?
12 What are the main features of simple random sampling?
13 What are the main attributes of systematic sampling?
14 What are the main differences between systematic sampling and simple random sampling.
15 Describe briefly the nature and use of 'sampling frames' in social research.
16 Explain the nature and use of the sampling fraction method.
17 Describe the nature and types of stratified sampling.
18 Explain the nature and use of cluster sampling.
19 Describe briefly the nature and purpose of multi-phase sampling.
20 Describe briefly the nature and purpose of multi-stage sampling.
21 What is an area sampling and how useful is it for social research?
22 What are panel studies, and how are they used in social research?
23 Describe briefly the differences between panel studies and trend studies.
24 Describe the nature and types of longitudinal studies.
25 What are the main problems of panel studies?
26 What are the main criteria of non-probability sampling?
27 What are the main types of non-probability sampling?
28 How is a sample chosen when the method of accidental sampling is used?
29 What is the nature and purpose of purposive sampling?
30 Describe briefly the selection of a sample when using the process of quota sampling.
31 Explain the nature and purpose of snowball sampling.
32 What are the main differences between quantitative and qualitative sampling procedures?
33 What are the main types of sampling that are employed in qualitative social research?
34 Describe briefly the process and purpose of theoretical sampling.
35 What are the main characteristics of sampling procedures employed by qualitative research?
36 What is meant by non-response in social research and how is it controlled?
37 What are the ways of estimating the ideal sample size?

Definitions of concepts

Define the following concepts:

Accidental sampling

....

Area sampling

....

Birthday methods

....

Cluster sampling

....

Complete coverage

....

Computer method

....

Dimensional sampling

....

First-letter method

....

Longitudinal studies

....

Lottery method

....

Multi-phase sampling

....

Multi-stage sampling

....

Non-probability sampling

....

Non-response

....

Number method

....

Panel studies

....

Primary selection units

....

Purposive sampling

....

Quota sampling

....

Random numbers

....

Random sampling

....

Sample

....

Sample size

....

Sampling fraction method

....

Sampling frame

....

Sampling procedures

....

Saturation

....

Saturation survey

....

Simple random sampling

....

Snowball sampling

....

Spatial sampling

....

Stratified random sampling

....

Survey population

....

Systematic sampling

....

Target population

....

Trend study

....

Multiple-choice questions

Answers to these multiple-choice questions are given at the end of the chapter.

1   The sampling procedure that includes all units of the population in the study is called
    a   complete coverage
    b   saturation survey
    c   survey population
    d   **a** and **b** above

2   Which of the following is *not* one of the principles of sampling listed in the text?
    a   Sampling units must be identifiable and clearly defined
    b   Sampling units must be representative and include males and females
    c   Sampling units are not interchangeable
    d   Sampling units must be independent from each other

3   Probability sampling is the procedure that gives all units
    a   a chance to be included in the study
    b   an equal chance to be selected
    c   an equal, calculable and non-zero chance to be selected
    d   **a** and **b** above

4   The types of probability sampling are
    a   random sampling, lottery method and snowball sampling
    b   random numbers, random sampling and computer methods
    c   computer methods, snowball sampling and lottery method
    d   simple random and systematic sampling

5 Three of the methods of unit selection in simple random sampling are
   a stratified sampling, quota sampling and accidental sampling
   b area sampling, multi-stage sampling and purposive sampling
   c cluster sampling, panel studies and accidental sampling
   d lottery method, computer method and random numbers method

6 In a stratified sampling, the strata
   a are equal in size to each other
   b are proportionate to the units in the target population
   c are disproportionate to the units in the target population
   d can be proportionate or disproportionate to the units in the target population

7 A cluster sampling is when
   a in the first instance groups of people are chosen for the study
   b a quota of people is chosen for the study
   c units are clustered together after the study to enhance data analysis
   d b and c above

8 In a multi-stage sampling
   a the same number of people are studied more than once
   b different respondents are studied more than once
   c a sequence of samples are drawn from already selected samples but only the last sample is studied
   d a sequence of samples is drawn from already selected samples and each one of them is studied

9 In a multi-phase sampling
   a the same number of people are studied more than once
   b different respondents are studied more than once
   c a sequence of samples are drawn from already selected samples but only the last sample is studied
   d a sequence of samples is drawn from already selected samples and each one of them is studied

10 Panel studies are
   a the same as longitudinal studies
   b studies in which different respondents are studied on more than one occasion on the same topic and using the same methods and questions
   c studies in which the same respondents are studied on more than one occasion
   d a and c above

11 Trend studies are
   a the same as longitudinal studies
   b studies in which different respondents are studied on more than one occasion on the same topic, and using the same methods and questions
   c studies in which the same respondents are studied on more than one occasion
   d a and b above

12   Spatial sampling is a sampling procedure in which
    a the sample is taken from people temporarily congregated in space
    b respondents are chosen through special systematic procedures
    c space is given particular consideration due to its nature
    d **a** and **d** above

13   Accidental sampling is the sampling procedure
    a in which respondents are chosen if they accidentally come in contact with the researcher
    b that is the same as incidental sampling
    c that is the same as incidental sampling and haphazard sampling
    d which entails all of the above

14   Most qualitative researchers
    a use sampling in their research
    b use non-probability sampling in their research
    c are critical of random sampling procedures
    d support all of the above

15   Theoretical sampling means that
    a sampling procedures follow theoretical principles
    b sampling is geared towards developing or testing a theory
    c each sampling procedure applies its own theory
    d none of the above is correct

16   Which of the following is *not* one of the criteria of qualitative sampling?
    a that all units have a fair chance to be selected in the study
    b that a few suitable units are included in the study
    c that a few typical cases are selected
    d that it is directed towards fewer global settings than quantitative sampling

17   With regard to qualitative research, which of the following is *not* correct?
    a qualitative researchers reject sampling as a tool of social research
    b qualitative researchers do not use sampling procedures
    c qualitative researchers do not plan sampling systematically
    d all of the above

18   A researcher entered a large restaurant and interviewed very briefly the oldest person sitting at every second table. This type of sampling is
    a systematic probability sampling
    b stratified sampling
    c spatial sampling
    d area sampling

19   A researcher interviewed the householder of two randomly selected houses in each of the streets of the Upper-Heights suburb of a town in South Australia. This sampling procedure is
    a probability sampling
    b stratified sampling
    c spatial sampling
    d area sampling

20 In a study of attitudes to university policies, a researcher questioned 150 first-year students 130 second-year students and 100 third-year students. The sampling procedure used in this study was
 a probability sampling
 b stratified sampling
 c spatial sampling
 d area sampling

21 In a study of attitudes to university policies, a researcher chose initially 150 first-year students, 130 second-year students and 100 third-year students (N_1=380). Then, the researcher chose 25 male and 25 female students from each year group who were finally interviewed (N_2=150). The sampling procedure used in this study was
 a probability sampling
 b stratified sampling
 c multi-stage sampling
 d multi-phase sampling

22 A researcher chose a sample by using a sampling frame and taking the person that corresponded to the kth number in the list. This procedure is called
 a simple random sampling
 b systematic sampling
 c stratified sampling
 d quota sampling

23 The sampling procedure in which an interviewer is asked to interview 25 young adults, 150 adults and 75 older persons is called
 a stratified sampling
 b accidental sampling
 c spatial sampling
 d quota sampling

24 The author ascertained the respondents of his cohabitation study by interviewing a few available cohabiting couples and by obtaining names of new couples from the previous respondents. This procedure is called
 a theoretical sampling
 b convenience sampling
 c snowball sampling
 d systematic sampling

25 A researcher chose the final 25 respondents by interviewing the two first respondents and choosing further respondents according to the information collected from each additional respondent. This sampling procedure is called
 a theoretical sampling
 b convenience sampling
 c snowball sampling
 d systematic sampling

Practical exercises

1   You have been asked to investigate the views of nurses working in hospitals in New South Wales with regard to whether health workers, and medical doctors in particular, should be allowed to strike or not. In this context, answer the following questions:

   a What is the most appropriate sampling procedure for this project and why?

   b How would you choose the respondents if the prescribed procedure was quota sampling?

2   In the above example, the research committee is interested in the interpretations nurses give to strikes and striking doctors. Explain how the nurses will be chosen if theoretical sampling is employed.

3   You have been appointed as the chief researcher of a country town. Your task is to ascertain the attitudes of unmarried mothers living in that community to state policies relating to family allowance.

   a Explain how you will choose the sample of mothers to address the research question, using a quantitative study.

   b Explain how you will choose the sample of mothers to address the research question, using a qualitative study.

4   As the research adviser of the educational division of the university you have been asked to investigate the views of students to the proposed increase in fees, which resulted from relevant government cuts. The sampling method you have been urged to use by the manager of the division is multi-stage sampling.

   a Describe the steps you will employ to select your respondents by using this method.

   b Discuss critically the suitability of such a sampling method in the context of the proposed study. Is this the sampling method you would have chosen if you had been free to decide on that matter?

Answers to multiple-choice questions

1 d	6 d	11 d	16 a	21 c
2 b	7 a	12 a	17 d	22 b
3 c	8 c	13 d	18 c	23 d
4 d	9 d	14 d	19 d	24 c
5 d	10 d	15 d	20 b	25 a

7

Methods of data collection: experiments and focus groups

Contents

Educational objectives

After completing this chapter, you will:

1　have a thorough knowledge of data collection and the way it is conducted;
2　have a clear understanding of how data collection is accomplished in both the quantitative and the qualitative domain of research;
3　know how experiments are conducted and how relevant data are assessed and used;
4　know how focus groups are employed as a means of data collection and how relevant data are assessed and used;
5　have a critical understanding of the process of data collection in general and the use of experiments and focus groups in particular.

Main points

The main points made in this chapter are:

1　Methods of data collection are often generic tools that can be employed in a variety of methodological contexts.
2　Qualitative methods are characterised by a number of criteria, related, among other things, to the nature of methodology, the relationship to the researched and the nature of the design.
3　Instrumentation before data collection is disputed by a number of researchers.
4　Triangulation is the procedure in which data collection is accomplished by more than one avenue.
5　Triangulation has a number of advantages and disadvantages.
6　Experiments involve the measurement of effects on a subject by controlling environmental factors and conditions.
7　Environmental factors and conditions are controlled through ruling out, closing off or controlling for a set of factors and conditions.
8　Experiments follow a set of steps. In a typical case experimentation involves a pre-test, a test and a post-test.
9　Sampling in experiments is accomplished by means of the methods of randomisation, subject matching and group matching.
10　There are several experimental designs employed in social research. Although they differ from each other, they all fall within the parameters of the standard research model introduced earlier in this volume.
11　Field experiments are new in social research but a growing method indeed.
12　The validity of experiments depends on a number of factors, some of which relate to maturation, conditioning and instrumentation, and others to the history effect, changes in samples, interaction, sampling, ecology, modelling or what is known as the Hawthorne effect.

13 Focus groups are usually employed in the areas of social work and less in other social sciences.
14 Focus groups facilitate collection of data by means of group discussion.
15 Group discussion is affected by a number of problems but if carefully employed it can be a useful tool of data collection.

Short-answer questions

Answer each question carefully. Consult your Social Research *text when your memory fails you or when you are in doubt about the accuracy of your responses.*

1 Explain in simple terms the nature and purpose of triangulation.
2 List the most serious criticisms of triangulation and discuss their methodological basis.
3 Explain in simple terms the nature and purpose of experiments.
4 What is meant by 'closure' when conducting experiments?
5 What are the main stages of experimental research?
6 How is sampling carried out in experimental research and how different is it from the standard sampling procedures employed in survey research?
7 How is 'randomisation' carried out in experimental research and what purpose does it serve?
8 Describe the process of data collection in experimental research?
9 What are the major types of experimental designs?
10 What are the major types of experiments?
11 Describe briefly the nature and purpose of demonstration experiments.
12 Explain the way in which field experiments are carried out and the purpose they serve.
13 Name the most important factors that can affect the validity of experiments.
14 Describe briefly the nature and purpose of 'group discussion'.
15 How is a focus group chosen in which 'discussion' is going to take place?
16 How is 'discussion' organised and controlled when 'group discussion' is carried out?
17 What is the role of the leader in the context of 'group discussion'?
18 List some of the problems that can affect group discussion.

Definition of concepts

Define the following concepts:

After-only design

....

Before-after experimental design

....

Classic experimental design

....

Closing off

....

Closure

....

Conditioning

....

Controlling for

....

Demonstration experiments

....

Ecology

....

Experiments

....

Field experiments

....

Focus groups

....

Group discussion

....

Group matching

....

Hawthorne effect

....

History effect

....

Instrumentation

....

Laboratory experiment

....

Maturation

....

Modelling

....

Post-test

....

Pre-test

....

Randomisation

....

Randomised group design

....

Ruling out

....

Subject matching

....

Triangulation

....

Multiple-choice questions

Answers to these multiple choice questions are given at the end of the chapter.

1 In qualitative research, closeness of the researcher means
   a that researchers are expected to work close to each other
   b that researchers come closer to reality and social interaction
   c both of the above
   d neither **a** nor **b**

2   In qualitative research, openness of the methods means
    a   that methods can be changed and adjusted during data collection
    b   that researchers can use methods at will
    c   that the choice of methods is not important for research outcomes
    d   none of the above

3   In qualitative research, 'communicative method' means
    a   that methods employ communicative means to capture the essence of interaction
    b   that methods use communication techniques to capture reality as objectively defined
    c   that methods are set to capture reality in communication and interaction
    d   **a** and **b** above

4   In qualitative research, 'naturalistic method' means
    a   methods as designed naturally by researchers
    b   methods employing natural techniques of data collection
    c   methods designed to study everyday life as it unfolds and is interpreted by the subjects
    d   methods applied in natural sciences

5   In qualitative research, instrumentation prior to the study is
    a   rejected as totally inadequate and ineffective
    b   accepted under certain conditions
    c   accepted by some researchers and rejected by others
    d   none of the above

6   Triangulation refers to the research technique that
    a   applies mathematical techniques (trigonometric) of analysis
    b   employs three samples of respondents (stratified or multi-stage sampling)
    c   employs several methods of data collection to answer the research question
    d   **b** and **c** above

7   Which of the following is *not* one of the criticisms levelled against triangulation?
    a   there is no evidence to suggest that triangulation produces more valid results
    b   single- and multiple-measure procedures can be equally useless
    c   triangulation is difficult to replicate
    d   it is more likely to cause researcher bias due to dealing with different methods

8   In experiments, the process of controlling the factors that influence the subjects is usually referred to as
    a   ruling out
    b   controlling for
    c   closing off
    d   all of the above

9   The method employed when choosing subjects for experiments is
    a   randomisation
    b   subject matching
    c   group matching
    d   all of the above

10 To assure a high degree of similarity between experimental and control
    groups the researcher
    a   employs subject matching techniques
    b   group matching techniques
    c   randomisation
    d   all of the above

11 Experimental and control groups are constructed by the researcher to be sim-
    ilar in
    a   gender, education and status
    b   factors related to the independent variable
    c   factors related to the dependent variable
    d   all of the above

12 Field experiments are characterised by the fact that
    a   they are performed in natural situations
    b   they use precautions employed in other types of experiments
    c   strict adherence to principles of experiments are often difficult to achieve
    d   all of the above

Practical exercises

1   You have been asked to investigate the effects of increased taxation on the
    spending patterns of working-class families. How will you design the study
    using triangulation?

2   Prepare a complete experimental research design to study the effects of the
    gender of interviewers on the response rate to door-to-door surveys.

3   Show how you will construct and employ focus groups as a tool of data col-
    lection when studying the views of persons of ethnic origin on female police
    officers.

Answers to multiple-choice questions

1 b	4 c	7 d	10 d
2 a	5 c	8 d	11 c
3 c	6 c	9 d	12 d

8

Field research and grounded theory

Contents

Educational objectives

After completing this chapter, you will:

1 have considered aspects of four newer methods of data collection and their application in social research;
2 have developed a good understanding of field research, its types and design, and the way it is employed in social sciences;
3 be familiar with the context, structure and application of case-study research as employed in quantitative and qualitative research;
4 have a good grounding in ethnographic research and its status in the social sciences;
5 be able to understand the basics of grounded theory research and its relevance to the discovery of knowledge;
6 have gained skills appropriate to conduct field research and critically assess its results;
7 have a critical understanding of the role of field research in the social sciences and its strengths and weaknesses.

Main points

The main points made in this chapter are:

1 Field research is a form of inquiry that takes place in the field and explores real-life situations as they unfold.
2 There are several types of field studies, for example, exploratory studies, descriptive studies and hypothesis-testing studies.
3 In principle, field study designs are similar to the standard research design explained earlier in this volume, only they are less complex and more flexible than quantitative designs.
4 A case study is defined as 'an empirical inquiry that investigates a contemporary phenomenon within its real-life context when the boundaries between phenomenon and context are not clearly evident, and where multiple sources of evidence are used'.
5 In qualitative research, case studies are often employed as the main form of inquiry.
6 In quantitative research, case studies are employed as a prelude to the main study, as a form of pre-test, or as a post-research explanation of the study.
7 A case-study protocol contains an overview of the case-study project, field procedures, case-study questions and a guide for preparing the report.
8 Ethnographic research was borrowed from ethnography and social anthropology and is used in the social sciences in a number of areas, for example, by feminists.
9 The main theoretical foundations of ethnographic research are culture, holism, in-depth studies and chronology.
10 The methods employed in ethnographic research are descriptive or critical; they are similar to those employed in other areas but ethnographic fieldwork and ethno-historic research are more characteristic of this type of research.

11 The purpose of ethnographic research depends on the underlying methodology being akin to positivistic and to critical research.
12 Grounded theory research falls within the parameters of qualitative research.
13 Grounded theory perceives research units as autonomous units, sees scientific interpretation of reality as the work of an artist, sees continuity from everyday thinking to scientific thinking and assumes openness of social scientific formation of concepts.

Short-answer questions

Answer each question carefully. Consult your Social Research *text when your memory fails you or when you are in doubt about the accuracy of your responses.*

1   Describe briefly the nature and purpose of field research.
2   Name the types of field studies employed in social research.
3   Describe the main elements of a field design.
4   Define case studies in simple terms and explain their purpose in social research.
5   Describe the structure and purpose of case studies in quantitative and qualitative research.
6   Explain the structure and purpose of the case-study protocol.
7   Describe the research model employed in case-study research.
8   What is 'ethnographic research' and how is it employed in social research?
9   Explain in simple terms the theoretical foundations of ethnographic research.
10 Describe the structure, purpose and methods of ethnographic research.
11 What are the criteria of ethnographic research?
12 How suitable is ethnography for social research?
13 Give a clear description of what is meant by grounded theory.
14 What are the central criteria of grounded theory?
15 List the main procedures and elements of grounded theory research.
16 What is meant by 'concept-indicator model' in grounded theory?
17 Describe the nature and types of coding as employed in grounded theory.
18 What are 'key categories' in grounded theory research and how are they developed?
19 Explain the structure, process and purpose of theoretical sampling.
20 What is 'saturation', how does it work and how useful is it for social research?
21 Describe the nature, types and purpose of theoretical memos.

Definitions of concepts

Define the following concepts:

Axial coding

Case study

....

Coding

....

Concept-indicator model

....

Descriptive studies

....

Eclectic approach

....

Ethnographic field work

....

Ethnographic research

....

Experimental studies

....

Exploratory studies

....

Field design

....

Field research

....

Field work

....

Grounded theory

....

Holistic approach

....

Hypothesis-testing studies

....

Open coding

....

Saturation

....

Selective coding

....

Theoretical memos

....

Theoretical sampling

....

Multiple-choice questions

Answers to these multiple choice questions are given at the end of the chapter.

1   Case studies and ethnographic research are usually referred to as
  a field research
  b naturalistic research
  c low-constraint research
  d all of the above

2   Field research is characterised by
  a the fact that it is an inquiry into real-life situations
  b the fact that it takes place in a setting that is not established just for the purpose of research
  c the fact that its respondents do not always know that they are studied
  d all of the above

3   Field studies are
  a exploratory studies
  b descriptive studies
  c hypothesis-testing studies
  d all of the above

4   Which of the following is *not* correct?
  Case study analysis differs from other types of research because it
  a studies units in their totality and not parts of units

    b is interested in past events and not in contemporary phenomena
    c studies typical cases
    d none of the above

5   In quantitative research, case studies are employed
    a as a prelude to quantitative studies
    b as a form of pre-test
    c as a post-research explanation of the main study
    d in all forms listed above

6   According to Yin, which of the following methods is used to analyse data obtained through case studies?
    a pattern-matching
    b explanation building
    c time-series analysis
    d all of the above

7   The types of coding employed in grounded theory research are
    a axial coding, normative coding and selective coding
    b open coding, axial coding, and selective coding
    c theoretical coding, axial coding and open coding
    d all of the above

Practical exercises

1   Develop a research design to study wife bashing in a country town using ethnographic research.
    a What type of decisions are required to be made?
    b What sort of methods will be chosen?
    c What kind of arrangements will have to be made to facilitate this research?

2   Use case-study research to explain marital relationships of ethnic migrants in a country town. State the specific objectives of the study and explain how this method will be employed to meet these objectives.

3   Using grounded theory research, devise a research model to study the views of Anglican clergy on the ordination of women. Explain how such research will begin and what kind of decisions will be made to make such a project possible.

Answers to multiple-choice questions

1 d	3 d	5 d	7 b
2 d	4 b	6 d	

9

Observation

Contents

Educational objectives

After completing this chapter, you will:

1 understand the nature and diversity of observation and its usefulness as a method of research;
2 have knowledge of the strengths and weaknesses of observation as a method of data collection;

3   be familiar with the differences between observation and other methods of data collection;
4   be able to employ observation in practical situations in the various forms it appears in social research;
5   be in a position to assess the nature and quality of studies employing observation and a critical reader of relevant research findings.

Main points

The main points made in this chapter are:

1   Observation is the method of data collection that employs vision as the only technique of collection.
2   There are several types of observation, for example, naive, scientific, participant, non-participant, structured, unstructured, natural, laboratory, open, hidden, active, passive and direct and indirect observation.
3   The steps of the research model employed in observation are similar to those of the standard model introduced earlier in this volume.
4   Sampling procedures in observation are similar to general procedures in this area.
5   Given the nature of the method, the observer is expected to be well qualified and have the required skills.
6   As a method of data collection, observation appears in a number of ways, for example, as continuous observation, time-point observation, time-interval observation and event observation.
7   Observation is a unique method that can be employed in areas where other methods are unsuitable and therefore offers several advantages.
8   Problems of observation can relate to a number of issues, for example, the observer, the purpose of observation, the tools used, the categories of observation and the expectations of the researcher.

Short-answer questions

Answer each question carefully. Consult your Social Research *text when your memory fails you or when you are in doubt about the accuracy of your responses.*

1   Describe briefly the nature and purpose of observation and its relation to other methods of data collection such as surveys and indirect methods.
2   Describe the differences between naive and scientific observation.
3   Explain the differences between participant and non-participant observation.
4   Describe the differences between structured and unstructured observation.
5   In what ways is natural observation different from laboratory observation?
6   In what sense can observation be open or hidden?
7   Show the differences between active and passive observation.
8   How can observation be direct or indirect?
9   What steps does the process of observation include?

10   In what ways are the process of topic selection and research design in observation different from the steps of the research process applied in social research?
11   What are the required skills an observer should have to be effective and to avoid problems and distortions?
12   What kind of issues does the training of observers usually include?
13   How does the process of data collection take place when observation is used as the method?
14   What is the most effective way of recording data in an observation situation?
15   What are the main advantages and limitations of observation?
16   What are the major problems of observation?
17   In what ways can the observer be a source of problems?
18   In what ways can the purpose of observation become a source of errors?
19   What are the areas in which observation can be most effective in social research?
20   How can problems of ethics and objectivity be controlled in observation?

Definitions of concepts

Define the following concepts:

Active observation

....

Direct observation

....

Hidden observation

....

Indirect observation

....

Laboratory observation

....

Naive observation

....

Natural observation

....

Non-participant observation

....

Observation

....

Open observation

....

Participant observation

....

Passive observation

....

Scientific observation

....

Semi-structured observation

....

Structured observation

....

Unstructured observation

....

True/false questions

Answers to these true/false questions are given at the end of the chapter.

1   Observation is a method that can be employed to study all types of events or phenomena.
2   Scientific observation is the type of observation that is systematic, related to goals and subjected to tests and controls.
3   Participant observation is the type of observation in which respondents 'actively participate' in the study.
4   Observing children playing in the schoolyard through a window is an example of non-participant observation.
5   Structured observation employs a strict procedure and a set of well-defined categories, and is subjected to high levels of control.
6   Unstructured observation has no structure at all and its process is practically left up to chance.
7   When observation is conducted in a qualitative framework, sampling procedures are not relevant and are therefore not required.

Practical exercises

1   It is suspected that illegal drugs are being smuggled in some way into the local gaol, and government authorities are eager to find out how. Survey research and other means available have proven inadequate, and it has been decided that participant observation might be more effective in shedding some light on this area.
    a   Prepare a research design to show how such a study will be constructed, including details about collection, analysis and evaluation of data.
    b   What measures will be taken to assure adherence to ethical standards?

2   A company manager reported that in an open-room office where eight employees are working, conflicts and problems are quite common. As a result, staff morale and work output have been reduced significantly.
    a   Design a research model using observation as a method to find out more about the problem, its course, causes, extent and real consequences.
    b   What measures will be taken to assure adherence to ethical standards?

Answers to true/false questions

1 F	3 F	5 T	7 F
2 T	4 T	6 F	

10

Surveys: mail questionnaires

Contents

Educational objectives

After completing this chapter, you will:

1   be familiar with the nature and complexities of survey research;
2   have an understanding of the distinction between the various types of questionnaires and their relevance to social research;
3   have gained an appreciation of the strengths and weaknesses of questionnaires as methods of data collection and their relevance to social research;
4   have developed skills that will help with the construction and administration of questionnaires in a professional manner;

5   have a critical understanding and appreciation of the place of questionnaires in quantitative and qualitative research, and of their limitations.

Main points

The main points made in this chapter are:

1   Questionnaires are a form of survey: a written survey.
2   Questionnaires have many advantages over other methods of data collection.
3   Questionnaires have many limitations of which the researcher must be aware.
4   The main elements of a questionnaire are the cover letter, instructions and main body.
5   The cover letter contains, among other things, information about the objectives and significance of the study, about the research team and the sponsors, about why the respondent should complete the questionnaire, about assurance of anonymity and confidentiality, and about other parameters.
6   The main body of the questionnaire contains the questions to be answered.
7   The questionnaire format can be one of the following: funnel format, inverted funnel format, diamond format, X-format, box format and mixed format.
8   The questionnaire usually contains primary, secondary and/or tertiary questions.
9   Padding questions are 'breathers' set before or after sensitive questions.
10 Probes are questions that are employed to encourage the respondent to complete, expand or amplify information already given during the study.
11 Filter questions are general in nature and inquire about issues that will be taken up by later questions.
12 Contingency questions ask for specific information on matters addressed by filter questions.
13 Fixed-alternative questions are closed or pre-coded questions that offer a set of possible answers for the respondent to choose from.
14 Open-ended questions offer no response options to choose from but space for the respondent to write down the answer.
15 Open-ended and fixed-alternative questions have their advantages and limitations.
16 Response sets included in a fixed-alternative question must meet the following requirements: they must be accurate, exhaustive, and uni-dimensional, and must include mutually exclusive categories.
17 Particular attention must be given to the nature and structure of response sets.
18 Particular attention must be given to the question content and especially to composition, relevance, clarity and simplicity, level and type of language, and to the attitude conveyed through the question.
19 Particular attention must be given to the questionnaire format.
20 Questions are the last step in a series of translations, leading from the definition of the research topic to indicators and to question wording.

Short-answer questions

Answer each question carefully. Consult your Social Research *text when your memory fails you or when you are in doubt about the accuracy of your responses.*

1 What are the advantages and limitations of questionnaires?
2 What are the main points that are expected to be included in a cover letter?
3 Describe briefly the structure and types of questionnaire formats.
4 Explain the nature and purpose of primary, secondary and tertiary questions.
5 What is the purpose of indirect questioning?
6 Explain the nature and purpose of suggestive questioning.
7 What are the differences between fixed-alternative and open-ended questions?
8 When are open-ended questions usually employed?
9 When are fixed-alternative questions normally used?
10 What are filter questions and when are they used?
11 What are contingency questions?
12 What are the three basic standards of constructing a response set in a questionnaire?
13 List five common types of response employed in questionnaires with fixed-alternative questions.
14 Describe five criteria that are important in defining the content of questions.
15 What are the rules of questionnaire construction that pertain to questionnaire layout?
16 Describe the main rules related to the construction of the content of questionnaires.
17 Describe the main rules related to the construction of the questionnaire format.
18 What are the most common steps of questionnaire construction?
19 What are the points that are commonly considered when reviewing a questionnaire?
20 Which aspects of questionnaires are incompatible with the principles of qualitative research and why?

Definitions of concepts

Define the following concepts:

Constant-sum scale

....

Contingency questions

....

Controlled directive probing

....

Cover letter

....

Direct questions

....

Face scales

....

Filter questions

....

Fixed-alternative questions

....

Graphic response

....

Indirect questions

....

Ladder scale

....

Likert scale

....

Numerical response

....

Padding questions

....

Primary questions

....

Probes

....

Prompts

....

Questionnaire format

....

Questionnaires

....

Ranking scales

....

Secondary questions

....

Suggestive questions

....

Summary technique

....

Tertiary questions

....

Thermometer scale

....

Uni-dimensionality

....

Verbal scales

....

Multiple-choice questions

Answers to these multiple choice questions are given at the end of the chapter.

1   Which of the following is correct?
    a surveys are the most popular methods of data collection in the social
       sciences
    b surveys are employed primarily by quantitative researchers
    c surveys include the use of questionnaires and interviewing
    d all of the above

2   Which of the following is *not* one of the advantages of questionnaires?
    a they offer a greater assurance of anonymity than many other methods
    b they are not affected by problems of 'non-contacts'
    c they offer lower consistency and uniformity than other methods
    d they produce quick results

3   Which of the following is *not* one of the limitations of questionnaires?
    a it is not possible to check whether the question order was followed
    b they do not allow probing and prompting
    c they offer a less considered and objective view on the issue in question than interviews
    d partial response is possible

4   Questions that are not central to the research topic but aim to encourage the respondent to complete, amplify or expand information given are called
    a probes
    b padding questions
    c prompts
    d filter questions

5   Which of the following is *not* one of the criteria of a response set?
    a that the response categories are exhaustive
    b that the response categories are adequately numbered to allow statistical analysis
    c that the response categories are mutually exclusive
    d that the response categories are uni-dimensional

6   The purpose of probes is to
    a help provide a complete answer
    b help amplify or expand collected information
    c guide the discussion
    d all of the above

7   The technique employed in probing is
    a the summary technique
    b the controlled no-directive technique
    c directive probing
    d all of the above

8   Which of the following is *not* one of the advantages of open-ended questions?
    a they allow freedom to express feelings and thoughts
    b they offer information not directly related to the question
    c they offer more details than pre-coded questions
    d they allow for creativity, self-expression and initiative

9 A general question (for example, 'Do you read the Bible?') followed by another more specific question (for example, 'How often do you read the Bible?') is
   a a primary
   b a prompt
   c a filter question
   d a probe

10 A specific question (for example, 'How often do you read the Bible?') that usually follows another more general question (for example, 'Do you read the Bible?') is
   a a primary
   b a secondary
   c a filter question
   d a contingency question

11 The question: 'The international Committee on Health Issues found that marijuana smoking increased the levels of cholesterol among females. Don't you also think that marijuana smoking affects cholesterol levels?'
   a includes suggestive questioning
   b entails prestige bias
   c is double-barrelled
   d is a and b above

12 Which of the following is *not* one of the criteria employed by most researchers when determining the content of questions?
   a relevance
   b symmetry
   c clarity
   d none of the above

13 Which of the following is *not* one of the criteria that are expected to be met when assessing the layout of questionnaires?
   a questions must be easy to read and easy to follow
   b sufficient space must be provided between the questions
   c questions should reflect clearly the essence of the topic they are supposed to address
   d sufficient space should be provided after open-ended questions for the respondent's comments

14 Which of the following is *not* one of the criteria that are expected to be observed when deciding about the content of questions?
   a questions must be relevant to one or more aspects of the study (except in case of secondary and tertiary questions)
   b ambiguous questions should be excluded from the questionnaire
   c threatening questions should not be included in the questionnaire
   d none of the above

Practical exercises

1   You have been working on a study of domestic violence in a small country
    town and wish to use home-delivered questionnaires for the collection of the
    data. The issue is interesting and topical but very sensitive.
    a Devise a cover letter to accompany the questionnaire and explain and jus-
    tify its main elements.
    b Devise a questionnaire and explain the reason for including each of the
    questions considered.

2   Explain where and how ethical standards can be violated through this study.

Answers to multiple-choice questions

1 d	**4** a	**7** d	**10** d	**13** c
2 c	**5** b	**8** b	**11** d	**14** d
3 c	**6** d	**9** c	**12** d	

11

Surveys: interviewing

Contents

Educational objectives

After completing this chapter, you will:

1 be familiar with the nature and complexities of survey research;
2 have an understanding of the distinction between the various types of interview and their relevance to social research;

3   have gained an appreciation of the strengths and weaknesses of interviews as methods of data collection and their relevance to social research;
4   have developed skills that will help with the construction and administration of interviews in a professional manner;
5   have a critical understanding and appreciation of the place of interviews in quantitative and qualitative research, and of their limitations.

Main points

The main points made in this chapter are:

1   Interviews are surveys conducted orally.
2   Interviews can be structured or unstructured, depending on the degree to which interviewers have to adhere to prescribed strict guidelines.
3   Interviews can be standardised or unstandardised; the former contain fixed alternative questions, the latter open-ended questions.
4   Individual interviews include one respondent at a time; group interviews include interviews with groups of people.
5   Other-administered and self-administered interviews vary according to who administers the interview.
6   Unique interviews are conducted once; panel interviews are repeated more than once.
7   Open interviews are unstructured and unstandardised interviews.
8   Ethnographic interviews involve key informants who convey information about the research question.
9   Delphi interviews are ethnographic interviews conducted in stages and involving the participation of the respondents in data collection and analysis.
10 Focused interviews are interviews focusing on a specific topic, which is presented through a stimulus such as a film, a written report or a situation.
11 Narrative interviews introduce a topic for discussion and encourage the respondent to offer as much information as possible.
12 Intensive interviews are mostly unstructured and unstandardised, aiming at an in-depth exploration of the issues in question.
13 In qualitative research, interviews are single and personal, employ open-ended questions and are open and flexible.
14 The tasks of the interviewer are, among other things, to choose the respondents (in quota sampling), arrange the interview conditions, ask the questions, control the interview situation, avoid bias, record the answers and guard the principles of ethics.
15 Choosing interviewers to be similar in background with respondents not only makes entry into the world of respondents easier but also promotes trust, mutual understanding and cooperation and therefore reduces bias and distortion.
16 Telephone interviewing produces quick results, can study large samples, is relatively economical, promotes open communication, reduces bias and guarantees more anonymity than face-to-face interviews.
17 Telephone interviews have a high refusal rate, cannot control the identity of the respondent or the interview process overall, and cannot address all possible respondents (for example, those without a telephone, or with unlisted numbers).

18 Interviews have many advantages and limitations of which the researcher must be aware when deciding on the appropriate method of data collection.
19 Interviews can now be carried out via computers. CAPI and CODSCI are two examples of computer-driven interviews.
20 Errors in interviewing can be associated with recording of data, evaluation of responses and instructions given to interviewers.

Short-answer questions

Answer each question carefully. Consult your Social Research *text when your memory fails you or when you are in doubt about the accuracy of your responses.*

1   List the major types of interviews.
2   What are the differences between structured and unstructured interviews?
3   What are the advantages and limitations of interviews?
4   What are the main criteria of standardised and unstandardised interviews?
5   Explain the nature and purpose of unique and panel interviews.
6   Describe the nature and purpose of open interviews.
7   Describe the nature and purpose of analytical interviews.
8   Describe the nature and purpose of diagnostic interviews.
9   Describe the nature and purpose of structure or dilemma interviews.
10 Describe the nature and purpose of ethnographic interviews.
11 Describe the nature and purpose of Delphi interviews.
12 Describe the nature and purpose of clinical interviews.
13 Describe the nature and purpose of biographical interviews.
14 Describe the nature and purpose of problem-centred interviews.
15 Describe the nature and purpose of focused interviews.
16 Describe the nature and purpose of narrative interviews.
17 Describe the nature and purpose of intensive interviews.
18 Describe the nature and purpose of receptive interviews.
19 Describe the nature and purpose of convergent interviews.
20 Describe the nature and purpose of elite interviews.
21 What are the criteria of qualitative interviews?
22 What are the main tasks of the interviewer?
23 What are the standards of selection of interviewers?
24 What are the main elements of interviewer training?
25 In what ways can an interviewer bias the research process?
26 Explain the differences between probing and prompting.
27 What are the main types of probing?
28 What are the advantages and limitations of telephone interviewing?
29 Explain the ways in which computers can assist in the process of interviewing. Give examples of programs developed in this context.
30 What are the main problems/errors affecting interviewing?
31 In what ways can errors occur when recording interview data?
32 In what ways can errors occur when evaluating interview data?

Definitions of concepts

Define the following concepts:

Analytical interviews

....

Biographical interviews

....

Clinical interviews

....

Computer interviews

....

Convergent interviews

....

'The data collector'

....

Delphi interviews

....

Diagnostic interviews

....

Dilemma interviews

....

Elite interviews

....

Ethnographic interviews

....

Focused interviews

....

Guided interviews

....

Hard interviews

....

Informative interviews

....

Inquiring interviews

....

Intensive interviewing

....

Interviewer bias

....

Narrative interviews

....

Open interviews

....

Panel interviews

....

Personal interviews

....

Problem-centred interviews

....

Receptive interviews

....

Semi-structured interviews

....

Soft interviews

....

Structured interviews

....

Surveys

....

Telephone interviews

....

Unique interviews

....

Unstructured interviews

....

Multiple-choice questions

Answers to these multiple choice questions are given at the end of the chapter.

1   Structured interviews
    a   employ a guide that must be strictly followed
    b   allow no flexibility in presentation and administration
    c   both of the above
    d   none of the above

2   The type of interview in which the interviewee is given a story containing a decision problem that they are asked to solve is
    a   a diagnostic interview
    b   an analytical interview
    c   an 'inquiring' interview
    d   a dilemma interview

3   The type of interview including experts who are interviewed and later further consulted on more than one occasion is called
    a   a clinical interview
    b   a discursive interview
    c   a Delphi interview
    d   b and c above

4   Which of the following is one of the criteria of qualitative interviews?
    a   they use open-ended questions only
    b   question structure is not fixed but flexible
    c   they are usually single interviews, questioning one person at a time
    d   all of the above

5 Interviews have an advantage over questionnaires because they can handle more effectively
  a complex questions
  b questions that require reference to other sources
  c sensitive issues
  d all of the above

6 Interviews, as they are used in social research, differ from those employed in everyday life in that they are
  a prepared in a systematic way
  b controlled by the researcher
  c related to a specific research question
  d all of the above

7 Which of the following is *not* permitted in standardised interviewing?
  a to change the order of the questions
  b to repeat the questions liberally and at will
  c to change the question wording
  d all of the above

8 The type of interview in which the interviewer cannot change content, order, etc. of questions is a
  a standardised interview
  b structured interview
  c unstandardised interview
  d unstructured interview

9 Interviews in which respondents are interviewed only once are
  a individual interviews
  b unique interviews
  c personal interviews
  d all of the above

10 Which of the following is *not* a criterion of qualitative interviews?
  a reflexivity
  b naturalism
  c standardisation
  d none of the above

11 Which of the following is *not* one of the advantages of telephone interviewing?
  a produces quick results
  b can address large samples
  c has a low refusal rate
  d is relatively economical

12 Which of the following is *not* one of the disadvantages of telephone interviewing?
   a the identity of the respondents is not known
   b communication with the respondent is restricted due to the nature of the medium
   c some people have no telephones or have unlisted numbers
   d the interview environment cannot be fully controlled

13 Which of the following is *not* one of the advantages of interviewing?
   a flexibility
   b easy administration
   c opportunity to record spontaneous answers
   d low cost

Practical exercises

1 For an investigation of public attitudes to police brutality in Northern Newland (recently reported in the popular media) devise an interview guide, including probes, prompts and relevant instructions for interviewers.

2 To establish the needs of young people in a rural town, the council decided to conduct an interview with persons under 21 years of age. Your task is to develop a complete interview guide and arrange the interview conditions. Which type of interview is most suitable?

Answers to multiple-choice questions

1 c	4 d	7 d	10 c	12 b
2 d	5 c	8 b	11 c	13 d
3 d	6 d	9 b		

12

Indirect methods of data collection

Contents

Educational objectives

After completing this chapter, you will:

1   be familiar with the nature, types and purpose of indirect methods in social research;

2 have an understanding of the diversity of indirect methods and their place in quantitative and qualitative social research;

3 have gained an appreciation of the strengths and weaknesses of the various indirect methods and their similarities and differences;

4 have developed skills that will help with the design and use of the various indirect methods;

5 have a critical knowledge and understanding of content analysis and its relevance and limitations within quantitative and qualitative research;

6 be aware of the ethical issues involved in research employing indirect methods.

Main points

The main points made in this chapter are:

1 Indirect methods are the methods that help gather data without direct participation of the respondents. They are also called unobtrusive methods.

2 Examples of indirect methods are physiological methods, study of physical traces, document analysis, projective methods and concealed methods such as observation.

3 Physiological methods collect data related to a person's body to make conclusions about that person's behaviour, while this person is not aware of being investigated.

4 In disguised methods, the respondent is aware of being investigated but not of the way in which responses will be evaluated.

5 Examples of disguised methods are knowledge tests, personality questionnaires, perception tests, memory tests and fill-in tests.

6 In studies of physical traces researchers examine traces to learn about those who created the traces.

7 Documentary methods examine documents to determine behaviours and attitudes of people reported in the content of these documents.

8 Such documents are public documents, archival records, personal documents, administrative documents, formal studies and reports.

9 Documentary methods are very useful because of the following properties: retrospectivity, accessibility, spontaneity, low costs, high quality, possibility of re-testing and non-reactivity.

10 Documentary methods do have certain limitations of which the researcher must be aware when deciding about using them in a project.

11 The biographical method entails the study of personal and biographical documents.

12 Biographical (and other) documents are analysed by means of one (or more) of the following: holistic method, particularistic method, comparative method, content analysis, quantitative method and classification method.

13 Content analysis is a documentary method that examines the (manifest or latent) content of documents.

14 In content analysis, data collection concentrates on presence, frequency, prominence, direction and intensity of the research units.

15 In content analysis, data collection is facilitated by means of categories.

16 In content analysis, quantitative data analysis is conducted by means of a descriptive analysis, categorical analysis, valence and intensity analysis, contingency analysis and contextual analysis.

17 In content analysis, qualitative data analysis is conducted by means of an analysis based on summary, explication, structuration, objective hermeneutics and latent structures of meaning.

18 Projective methods examine 'trivial' aspects of behaviour in order to understand deeper feelings, emotions and problems.

19 Projective methods are employed predominantly by psychologists.

20 Indirect methods are employed as the only methods of study or in conjunction with other methods.

Short-answer questions

Answer each question carefully. Consult your Social Research *text when your memory fails you or when you are in doubt about the accuracy of your responses.*

1 In what ways are indirect methods 'indirect'?

2 What are the advantages of indirect methods in social research?

3 What are the major types of indirect methods?

4 Are indirect methods employed in quantitative research, qualitative studies or in both? Explain your answer.

5 How can the use of 'psychological' methods in social research be justified?

6 What are 'primary' and 'secondary' physiological methods and how are they used in social research?

7 How is the study of traces employed in the area of social research? Give examples.

8 What are the strengths and weaknesses of the study of traces?

9 What are 'documentary methods' and how can they be used in social research?

10 Are documentary methods primarily quantitative or qualitative in nature?

11 What are the most common types of documents considered in documentary research?

12 What are the major forms of documentary research?

13 What are the major advantages and limitations of documentary research?

14 How relevant is the biographical method to social research? How does it operate?

15 What are the major methods of analysis of biographical documents?

16 Is the biographical method a tool of qualitative or quantitative research?

17 What is 'content analysis' and what is its structure and purpose?

18 Is content analysis a quantitative or a qualitative method?

19 What are 'categories' and how are they used in content analysis? Give examples.

20 What are the major steps of category construction in content analysis?

21 What are the methods and techniques of data analysis employed by quantitative researchers in content analysis?

22 How is the method of objective hermeneutics employed in the analysis of qualitative data gathering through content analysis?

23 What are 'projective methods' and how can they be used in social research?

24   What are the types of projective methods employed in social research?
25   How are 'fill-in' methods used in social research and how useful are their findings? Give examples.
26   How are 'comic-strip' tests employed in social research and how useful are their findings? Give examples.
27   How are 'game tests' employed in social research and how useful are their findings? Give examples.
28   In what areas can indirect methods violate the rules of objectivity and how can this be remedied (assuming that objectivity is to be observed)?
29   How can indirect methods violate ethics and how can they be used to avoid this problem?
30   When and how can indirect methods assist in solving social problems in modern societies?
31   Does the employment of indirect methods enrich social research? Explain why.
32   If you were to criticise indirect methods, which elements would you criticise most and in what way?
33   How valid is data obtained through indirect methods?

Definitions of concepts

Define the following concepts:

Comic-strip test

....

Concealed methods

....

Constructive method

....

Content analysis

....

Count test

....

Disguised methods

....

Exemplification method

....

Explication

....

Frequency analysis

....

Game tests

....

Non-reactive methods

....

Non-reactivity

....

Objective hermeneutics

....

Physical traces

....

Physiological methods

....

Projective methods

....

Retrospectivity

....

Rorschach test

....

Spontaneity

....

Structuration

....

Thematic apperception tests

....

Typological analysis

....

Valence analysis

....

Wartegg-Zeichen Test

....

Multiple-choice questions

Answers to these multiple-choice questions are given at the end of the chapter.

1   Which of the following is a disguised method of data collection:
    a knowledge tests
    b perception tests
    c memory tests
    d all of the above

2   Disguised methods are
    a direct methods
    b indirect methods
    c physiological methods
    d documentary methods

3   The study of physical traces is a form of
    a direct methods
    b indirect methods
    c physiological methods
    d documentary methods

4   Which of the following is a form of documents employed in documentary research?
    a public records
    b archival records
    c diaries and autobiographies
    d all of the above

5   Which of the following is *not* one of the advantages of documentary methods?
    a retrospectivity
    b spontaneity
    c high reliability
    d non-reactivity

6 Which of the following is *not* one of the weaknesses of content analysis?
   a lack of access to some documents (personal diaries etc.)
   b incompleteness of some documents
   c high costs
   d lack of representativeness

7 The method in which respondents are given 31 black-and-white pictures and are asked to write a story for each picture is called
   a fill-in method
   b thematic apperception test
   c association test
   d none of the above

8 Projective methods are a type of
   a direct method
   b indirect method
   c physiological method
   d documentary method

9 Content analysis is a
   a direct method
   b indirect method
   c physiological method
   d projective method

10 Content analysis is a
   a quantitative method
   b qualitative method
   c both, depending on the research design
   d is not clear

Practical exercises

1 Devise a research design to investigate rural crisis in the 1970s in New South Wales by using content analysis as a method. Explain how this issue will be conceptualised and approached, how categories will be developed, and how the findings will be analysed and interpreted.

2 Explain how the study of traces can help study domestic violence. Develop a research model to explore this issue.

3 You are using comic-strip tests to investigate the attitudes of primary school children to class management techniques and gender differences on this issue. Describe three comic strips that, in your opinion, may assist in this context.

Answers to multiple-choice questions

1 d	3 b	5 c	7 b	9 b
2 b	4 d	6 c	8 b	10 c

13

Data collection

Contents

Educational objectives

After completing this chapter, you will:

1 understand the process of data collection as it happens in practical situations;
2 have studied the details of arrangements made for the collection of data within the various methods employed for that purpose;

3   be in a position to collect data and make decisions that will facilitate this process;
4   be able to assess the quality of the process of data collection conducted by other researchers;
5   be able to identify strengths and weaknesses of proposals regarding data collection and make appropriate decisions;
6   have a critical understanding of the process of data collection and of the effects it may have on the quality of findings.

Main points

The main points made in this chapter are:

1   Pre-tests are small tests of single elements of the research instruments, aiming to check their soundness and relevance.
2   Pilot study is a small-scale replica of the main study including a fraction of the sample.
3   Pre-tests mainly address research instruments, pilot studies mainly address research process and outcomes.
4   The overall process of data collection in quantitative and qualitative research is similar.
5   Data collection by means of interviewing entails advertising for, choosing and training interviewers, arranging work conditions for personnel, arranging for the interviewers to conduct interviews, supervising interviewers, and collecting data and checking interviews for completeness.
6   Non-response in questionnaires is a serious matter that has to be dealt with satisfactorily for both the respondents and the project.
7   Researchers have developed a set of rules that must be considered if a high response rate is to be achieved.
8   In documentary methods data collection proceeds as in other methods, that is, it involves identification of the documents and examination of their structure, content, etc. by means of categories or other instruments.
9   In observational research, data collection entails establishing contact with the subjects, conducting the observation, recording the data and observing the rules of ethics.
10   In experimental research, data collection entails establishing the experimental conditions and pre-testing, testing and post-testing them as the experimental model prescribes.
11   In field experiments, data collection proceeds as follows: identify the field, arrange the experimental conditions, induce stimulus as required and record the results.
12   In case study research, the nature of data collection depends on the method(s) chosen for that purpose (interviews, documents, observation, etc.). Data collection using these methods has already been discussed.
13   Data collection is expected to meet certain general principles, such as maintaining objectivity, observing the code of ethics, being accurate and systematic, seeing data collection as a part of the research process (not an end in itself), following the instructions of the researcher, avoiding errors and distortions, and being fair and honest.

Short-answer questions

Answer each question carefully. Consult your Social Research *text when your memory fails you or when you are in doubt about the accuracy of your responses.*

1   What are pre-tests and pilot studies?
2   What are the major differences between pre-tests and pilot studies?
3   When are pre-tests and pilot studies employed?
4   What are the major differences between the processes of data collection in a qualitative and quantitative context?
5   What does data collection involve when interviewing is the main instrument of collection?
6   Describe the process of data collection in studies employing telephone interviewing as their main instrument.
7   How is non-response addressed in social research? What is the task of the researcher?
8   How can non-response be reduced or avoided?
9   List five ways that can help reduce or avoid non-response.
10 What are the main tasks to be accomplished in order to collect data in observational research?
11 Explain briefly the steps that are followed in experimental studies in order to collect data.
12 Describe the process of data collection in investigations employing case studies as their method of data collection.

Definition of concepts

Define the following concepts:

Closure

....

Data collection

....

Non-response

....

Pilot studies

....

Pre-tests

....

Qualitative analysis

....

True/false questions

Answers to these true/false questions are given at the end of the chapter.

1   A pre-test is a small-scale replica of the major study, and is predominantly used to check eventual 'mechanical' problems of the study.
2   A pre-test aims to establish the suitability and effectiveness of a particular research instrument.
3   A pilot study aims, among other things, to gain information about how diverse the target or survey population is.
4   Pilot studies are very useful, particularly with regard to qualitative research.
5   In principle, there are no differences in data collection between quantitative and qualitative studies.

Practical exercises

1   You have designed a quantitative investigation to study the effects of depression on the dropout rate of students attending New South Wales tertiary institutions. The method of data collection is a self-administered questionnaire. Explain how you will plan a pilot study and what information such a study will be able to offer.

2   You have been given the task of investigating husband abuse and especially the construction of violence as experienced by husbands as victims. The method of data collection is intensive interviewing. Explain how you will address this problem, what arrangements you will make to collect the information and what precautions you will take to assure that the information you gather is genuine.

Answers to true/false questions

1 F   2 T   3 T   4 F   5 T

14

Analysis and interpretation

Contents

Educational objectives

After completing this chapter, you will:

1 understand the process of data analysis in qualitative and quantitative research;
2 have studied the types of analysis that are employed in social research and be able to assess their strengths and weaknesses;
3 be in a position to recognise the limits of data analysis and to evaluate the significance of the findings for the community;
4 have a clear understanding of the debate about the nature of data analysis and be able to respond intelligently to the various points made in the debate;
5 have developed a clear understanding of the use of computers during the process of analysis and be aware of their strengths and weaknesses;
6 be in a position to enter data in the computer using SPSS.

Main points

The main points made in this chapter are:

1 Quantitative and qualitative research employ different types of data analysis.
2 For a number of qualitative researchers, analysis is a cyclical and not a linear process.
3 For a number of qualitative researchers, data analysis takes place during and after data collection.
4 Overall, data analysis in qualitative research is not as clear and uniform as it is in quantitative research.
5 In qualitative interviews one possible way of data analysis entails transcription, checking and editing, analysis and interpretation, generalisations and verifications.
6 In case-study research, data analysis can be accomplished by one or more of the following methods: pattern-matching, explanation-building techniques, time-series analysis, making repeated observations and secondary analysis
7 According to one view of qualitative research, interpretation includes the following tactics: noting patterns or themes, seeing plausibility, clustering, making metaphors, counting, making contrasts/comparisons, partitioning variables, subsuming particulars into general, factoring, noting relationships between variables, finding intervening variables, building a logical chain of evidence and making conceptual and theoretical coherence.
8 Many qualitative researchers do not employ mathematical/statistical methods in data analysis. Others do.
9 Qualitative researchers extensively employ computers in data analysis. Several computer programs have been developed to aid with qualitative data analysis.
10 Computers are used in qualitative research for recording and storing, coding, retrieving and linking data, and displaying and integrating data.
11 There are three types of quantitative analysis: primary analysis, secondary analysis and meta-analysis.

12 Primary analysis refers to original, first-hand information.
13 Secondary analysis relates to already existing (second-hand) information.
14 Meta-analysis is a type of secondary analysis that attempts to standardise existing findings so that they can offer an integrated answer to the research question.
15 Quantitative data analysis entails data preparation, counting, grouping and presentation, relating, significance testing and predicting.
16 Electronic data processing is very common and a preferred option because it is fast, complete, accurate and effective.
17 Entering data in the computer begins with naming the variables, variable labels and values.

Short-answer questions

Answer each question carefully. Consult your Social Research *text when your memory fails you or when you are in doubt about the accuracy of your responses.*

1 What are the major elements of qualitative analysis?
2 What are the main types of coding in qualitative research?
3 Describe the differences between open, axial and selective coding.
4 Describe briefly the methods of qualitative analysis as presented by Neuman.
5 Describe the methods of qualitative analysis as given by Miles and Huberman.
6 How is qualitative analysis done when data collection is accomplished through qualitative interviews? Is the process of analysis involved here compatible with the standards and principles of qualitative research?
7 Are statistical measures employed in qualitative analysis?
8 Describe briefly the main points of the process of quantitative analysis.
9 How are computers employed in quantitative research and for what purpose?
10 What are the advantages of using computers in social research?
11 List five differences between quantitative and qualitative analysis.
12 What does the process of data preparation involve in quantitative analysis?
13 Explain how coding helps prepare data for quantitative analysis.
14 Describe the process of processing open-ended questions for analysis.
15 Describe briefly the process of counting and tallying as elements of quantitative analysis.

Definitions of concepts

Define the following concepts:

Analytic comparison

....

Axial coding

....

Checking

....

Code book

....

Coding

....

Counting

....

Cultural analysis

....

Domain analysis

....

Editing

....

The ethnograph

....

Explanation-building technique

....

Ideal types

....

Illustrative method

....

Manual preparation

....

Method of agreement

....

Method of difference

....

Open coding

....

Paper cards

....

Paper tapes

....

Pattern matching

....

Post-coding

....

Pre-coding

....

Selective coding

....

Storing

....

Successive approximation

....

Tallying the frequencies

....

Time-series analysis

....

Practical exercises

1   An attitude survey of 560 third-year social sciences students including 58
     questions has been completed and you are ready to enter the data in the com-
     puter. The first five survey questions were:
     Question 1:   age (years)
     Question 2:   gender (male, female)
     Question 3:   place of birth (country, city)

Question 4:   degree of satisfaction with student union facilities (rated as very high, high, moderate, low, and very low)

Question 5:   degree of satisfaction with the level of university fees (rated: very high, high, moderate, low, and very low)

Your task is to enter the data in the computer and, first of all, to define the variables, that is, to set up the framework in which the data will be placed. To accomplish this you will have to:

a   name the variables;
b   specify the variable label;
c   specify the values; and
d   specify the missing values.

The computer program employed here is SPSS.

2   In the above example, the answers of the first 20 students to the first five questions are shown below:

Question 1:   21, 24, 23, 21, 22, 21, 21, 25, 23, 21, 23, 22, 21, 21, 21, 23, 21, 22, 23, 21.

Question 2:   male, male, female, female, female, female, male, male, female, female, female, female, male, male, male, female, male, male, male, female.

Question 3:   city, city, country, city, city, city, country, city, city, country, country, city, city, city, country, country, city, city, country, city.

Question 4:   low, low, moderate, low, low, moderate, low, very high, low, very high, high, very low, low, moderate, low, low, high, very high, moderate.

Question 5:   moderate, moderate, low, high, high, moderate, moderate, low, high, moderate, moderate, low, low, high, low, high, high, moderate, low, very high.

Having named the variables, your task is now to enter the responses in the computer.

3   A study of 380 families investigated the relationship between religious observance and family wellbeing. The table published in a journal article is reproduced below.

Religious observance and family wellbeing

Family wellbeing	High observance	Moderate observance	Low observance
High	67	32	21
Moderate	42	58	17
Low	13	61	69
Total	122	151	107

You now wish to run a few tests to establish whether there is a relationship between the variables in question. For this you need to enter that data in the computer. Given that the data is given in a tabular form, how can you accomplish this task?

Hint: Firstly you name the variables (wellbeing, religiosity, count), and specify their values. Then you set the figures in the columns. The arrangement of the table figures shown below may help you with this task.

1	1	67
1	2	32
1	3	21
2	1	42
2	2	58
2	3	17
3	1	13
3	2	61
3	3	69

Apply the steps shown in your text to instruct the computer how to set the data in the table and how to treat these numbers when computations are made.

15

Data presentation

Contents

Educational objectives

After completing this chapter, you will:

1 have an understanding of the nature, types and purpose of tables and graphs as employed in quantitative and qualitative research;
2 be able to interpret and construct tables and graphs;
3 be aware of the complexity of forms of data presentation and of their strengths and limitations;
4 have a critical understanding of the use of tables and graphs in qualitative and quantitative research;
5 have the computer skills that are required to construct tables and graphs (using SPSS).

Main points

The main points made in this chapter are:

1   Frequency distributions present the frequency of occurrence of observations in a range of scale values.
2   Percentage distributions present values in percentages.
3   There are univariate, bivariate and multivariate tables.
4   Tables usually include a title, a heading, a body, marginals and footnotes.
5   Table presentation is expected to adhere to rules of clarity, simplicity, economy of space, order of variables, appearance, accuracy and objectivity.
6   Tables can be constructed by using computers.
7   Graphs present data visually. Most graphs are constructed within the framework of the coordinate axes; the X-axis (abscissa) and the Y-axis (ordinate).
8   Independent variables are scaled along the abscissa. Dependent variables are scaled along the vertical axis, the ordinate.
9   Frequency polygons, histograms and bar graphs are popular types of graphs.
10   Scattergrams are more complex and are used to demonstrate associations between variables.
11   Pie charts and cartographs are equally popular; they are not constructed around the coordinate axes.
12   Pictographs and population pyramids are additional examples of graphs.
13   Stem and leaf displays allow visual detailed presentation of trends in relatively small sets of data.
14   Graphs can be conveniently constructed by the computer.
15   Graphs are common in qualitative research. Examples are matrices, figures and charts.

Short-answer questions

Answer each question carefully. Consult your Social Research *text when your memory fails you or when you are in doubt about the accuracy of your responses.*

1   What is the purpose of data presentation (goals, functions, meaning)?
2   In what way do distributions present data?
3   What are the main types and elements of a table and how are tables used in social research?
4   What are the main rules of table presentation in social research?
5   What is the purpose of presenting data in graphs?
6   What are the main types of graphs?
7   Describe the similarities and differences of histograms and frequency polygons.
8   What is the purpose of visual presentation of data and what are some of the features they demonstrate? Use pie graphs, population pyramids and cartographs as examples.
9   Describe the main features and types of stem and leaf displays.

Definitions of concepts

Define the following concepts:

Area diagrams

....

Bar graphs

....

Bivariate tables

....

Body diagrams

....

Cartographs

....

Cells

....

Class interval

....

Class limits

....

Class range

....

Class width

....

Cumulative distributions

....

Distributions

....

Frequency distributions

....

Frequency polygon

....

Graphs

....

Histogram

....

Marginals

....

Matrices

....

Midpoint

....

Multivariate tables

....

Normal curve

....

Ogives

....

Open-ended class

....

Picture diagrams

....

Pie graphs

....

Population pyramids

....

Profiles

....

Scattergrams

....

Stem and leaf display

....

Tables

....

Univariate tables

....

Practical exercises

1 A recent study of single mothers who were members of the *Flower Club* and who had children under 8 years of age, produced the following findings:

Child's age	Number of children
1	12
2	65
3	31
4	28
5	17
6	12
7	8
8	4

The following tasks are to be accomplished:
a display these figures in a frequency distribution;
b construct a bar graph; and
c construct a histogram.

These tasks can be accomplished manually or by means of computers. Obviously the latter is often the preferred option. Task **a** is to be done manually, anyway, and this is the one that is required before the others.

Hint: You cannot use the computer, unless the data has already been entered! To do this, you have to set the figures in one column containing the children according to their age. This means that this column will contain 12 times the number 1, 65 times the number 2, 31 times the number 3 etc. When all data is in the column (under a well-defined variable), you proceed with the next step (see *Social Research* text for details).

2   In a methodology class of 68 students the final grades were distributed as follows: 14 per cent of the students obtained a high distinction, 18 per cent a distinction, 27 per cent a credit, 36 a pass and 5 per cent failed. Display these figures in a pie graph.

3   The individual test marks in the end of session examination Sociology 1 were as follows:

56, 34, 78, 98, 75, 86, 81, 67, 73, 69, 65, 86, 91, 58, 95, 78, 55, 84, 54, 73, 58, 77, 94, 66, 69, 63, 86, 72, 74, 83, 59, 88, 62, 82, 66, 46, 87, 49, 95, 48, 67, 48, 97, 49, 63, 56, 90, 68.

Construct a stem and leaf display to present these findings. Use a double-stem display.

4   A group of 30 graduates of 10 universities were asked to state the year in which they graduated. The years were 1995, 1996 and 1997. The table below shows row figures for the year of graduation and the number of graduates; the names of the universities were left out of the presentation.

Year	Number	Year	Number	Year	Number
1995	1	1996	2	1997	0
1996	3	1997	1	1996	1
1997	2	1995	0	1995	2
1997	2	1996	1	1997	1
1996	3	1997	2	1997	0
1995	2	1995	3	1995	2
1997	2	1996	4	1996	1
1996	1	1997	0	1997	3
1995	3	1996	2	1996	2
1995	0	1995	1	1995	1

a   Display the figures in a *stacked bar chart*.
b   Display the figures in a *clustered bar chart*.

How do you do that?

Hint: Follow the steps shown below:

i   Firstly, set the data in two columns, one for the years and one for the number of graduates (named 'Years' and 'Grads' respectively).

ii For stacked bar charts proceed as follows:
  a Choose Graphs>Bar
  b Click on **Stacked>Define**
  c Transfer 'Grad' to **Category Axis** box
  d Transfer 'Years' to **Define Stacks by** box
  e Click on **OK**

iii To obtain clustered bar charts proceed as follows:
   a Choose Graphs>Bar
   b Click on **Clustered>Define**
   c Transfer 'Grads' to **Category Axis** box
   d Transfer 'Years' to **Define Clusters by** box
   e Click on **OK**

In both cases the computer will display the respective charts.

Make sure that you always enter the data correctly, and that you define the variables accurately.

5 In the local early childhood centre, the age of children in group A ranges between 1 and 4 years. More specifically, the ages are 1, 3, 1, 2, 4, 1, 2, 1, 2, 2, 2, 1, 1, 3, 4, 2 and 1.

Display the age groups in a pie graph.

Hint: After having set the figures in a column named 'Child', proceed as follows:

a Choose Graphs>Pie
b Activate (that is, click on **O** in front of) **Summaries for Groups**
c Click on 'Define'
d Transfer 'Child' to **Define slices by** box
e Click on **Continue**
f Click on **OK**

You should now be able to construct other types of charts, such as line charts and area charts. The steps used are the same.

16

Central tendency and dispersion

Contents

Educational objectives

After completing this chapter, you will:

1   have a thorough understanding of the nature and purpose of measures of central tendency as employed in social research;
2   be able to identify the properties and distinguish the various types of measures and assess their relevance for data analysis;
3   be in a position to recognise the role of the measures of central tendency in quantitative and qualitative research;

4 have a critical understanding of the meaning of these measures for social research, and recognise their strengths, weaknesses and limitations;

5 have developed the relevant computer skills that are required to compute measures of central tendency and dispersion.

Main points

The main points made in this chapter are:

1 Relational measures relate parts of a group of scores to each other or to the whole group.

2 Rate relates values of different variables to each other.

3 Ratio relates parts of a variable to each other.

4 Percentage compares a part to the whole.

5 A mean describes the central trend or average of all observations.

6 Mode is the category of a distribution that has the largest number of observations.

7 Median is the point on a distribution that divides the observations (not their values) into two equal parts.

8 The mode can be used with nominal, ordinal, interval and ratio-level data.

9 The median can be used with ordinal, interval and ratio data.

10 The mean can be used with interval and ratio data only.

11 If the distribution is skewed, the median is to be used.

12 If the distribution is skewed and contains ordinal data, the mode is to be used.

13 The variance is the average of the squared deviations from the mean.

14 Standard deviation is the square root of the variance.

15 The range describes the distance between the lowest and the highest score in a distribution.

16 Interquartile range is the difference between the lowest score of the second quartile and the highest score of the third quartile.

17 Z-scores are (standardised) raw scores from different distributions that are converted into units of a common distribution that has a mean of 0 and a standard deviation of 1.

Short-answer questions

Answer each question carefully. Consult your Social Research *text when your memory fails you or when you are in doubt about the accuracy of your responses.*

1 What are the main relational measures employed in social research?

2 What are the main measures of central tendency employed in social research?

3 What are the main properties of the mean, median and mode?

4 When are the mean, the median or the mode supposed to be employed?

5 Which of the three measures of central tendency is the most effective?

6 Describe briefly the nature and purpose of the measures of dispersion.

7 Define variance and standard deviation and explain their purpose for social research.

8   Explain the relevance and adequacy of the range as a measure of variability in social research.
9   What is an interquartile range and how different is it from the range.
10 What are 'standard scores' and what is their purpose in social research?
11 Describe the nature and purpose of z-scores and their relationship to raw scores.
12 What is a *coefficient of variation* and what is its purpose?
13 What are the similarities/differences between z-scores and the coefficient of variation?

Definitions of concepts

Define the following concepts:

Coefficient of variation

....

Group data

....

Interquartile range

....

Listed data

....

Mean

....

Median

....

Mode

....

Percentage

....

Range

....

Rate

....

Ratio

....

Standard deviation

....

Standard scores

....

t-score

....

Variance

....

Practical exercises

1   The first year enrolment in a psychology class is 425 students, of which 31 are foreign students and the remaining Australian students. Compute the Australian/ foreign students' ratio and the percentage of foreign students in this class.

2   In the psychology class above, 201 students are female. What is the ratio of female to male students? What are the percentages of male and female students?

3   In the following data sets, compute the mean, mode and the median:

   Set A: 7, 5, 8, 9, 6, 7, 5, 3, 6, 4, 6, 8, 9, 7, 2, 5, 6, 7, 3, 6.

   Set B: 18, 21, 6, 22, 26, 23, 5, 4, 28, 5, 5, 20, 21, 27, 5.

   Which of these three measures is most appropriate for each set?

4   For the two data sets above compute the variance, standard deviation and the range. Compare these measures. What do the results tell you about the usefulness of these measures?

5   During the previous session, 15 students completed a subject in psychological methods and one in sociological methods. Their results (out of 10) were as follows:

   Psychology: 4, 6, 8, 7, 9, 4, 6, 5, 7, 6, 6, 7, 6, 5, 6.

   Sociology: 6, 8, 7, 9, 8, 7, 8, 6, 7, 4, 5, 3, 4, 7, 6.

   Compute the mean, range, standard deviation, and *z*-scores for both data sets. What do the findings tell you about the performance of these students? Do they do better in one of the study areas than in the other?

17

Associations

Contents

Educational objectives

After completing this chapter, you will:

1   have gained clear knowledge of the concept and use of correlations, and their role in social research;
2   be aware of the variety of measures of association and the differences between them;
3   have a critical understanding of the strengths and weaknesses of the measures of association and their theoretical and methodological limitations;

4 have gained the skills required to understand statistical findings of other researchers in this area and be able to critically assess their status and validity;
5 be able to assess the suitability of methods for particular research projects;
6 have developed the computer skills required to perform a statistical analysis in this area.

Main points

The main points made in this chapter are:

1 Correlations display the relationship between two variables.
2 Correlation coefficients demonstrate the presence or absence of correlation, the direction of correlation and the strength of correlation.
3 A correlation coefficient ranges from +1 to −1.
4 Association in nominally measured data can be computed by means of Yule's Q, contingency coefficient, Tschuprow's T, Cramer's V, and ϕ coefficient.
5 Association in ordinally measured data can be computed by means of Spearman's rho (ρ), Tau-α, gamma coefficient, Sommer's d, and Tau-β.
6 Association in interval/ratio measured data can be computed by means of Pearson's r.
7 Yules Q operates on the principle that if values are set in a four-cell table, the cross-products of the internal diagonal cells will be equal when no relationship exists between the variables.
8 The ϕ coefficient is a measure of association that is normally used for 2×2 tables, and builds on the χ^2 value.
9 Cramer's V has the same properties as ϕ but in addition it can be used for tables larger than 2×2.
10 Spearman's rank order correlation coefficient is employed when data are ordinally measured.
11 Pearson's rank order correlation coefficient is suitable for interval/ratio measured data.
12 A positive correlation means that when one variable is increased the other will increase too.
13 A negative correlation indicates that an increase in one variable is associated with a decrease in the other.
14 A zero correlation means that there is no association between the variables.
15 A correlation is thought to be very low when the coefficient is under .20, and low if the coefficient is between .21 and .40.
16 A correlation is thought to be moderate if the coefficient is between .41 and .70.
17 A correlation is thought to be high if the coefficient is between .71 and .90 and very high if the coefficient is over .91.
18 Conventions regarding the labelling of the strength of correlations vary.
19 The coefficient of determination is the square of the coefficient of correlation and displays the degree of variability shared by the two variables.
20 Regression is a method that allows researchers to make predictions regarding one variable, if the value of another variable is known.

Short-answer questions

Answer each question carefully. Consult your Social Research *text when your memory fails you or when you are in doubt about the accuracy of your responses.*

1 Describe briefly the nature and purpose of correlation.
2 What kind of information can a correlation offer?
3 What are the major types of correlation measures employed in social research?
4 What are the measures of association that are suitable for nominal data?
5 Which correlation measures are suitable for ordinal data?
6 Which correlation measure is the most popular for interval/ratio data?
7 When is Yule's Q employed in social research?
8 What is the logic on which Yule's Q operates?
9 In what areas and for what purpose is Spearman's rho employed?
10 When and under what conditions is Pearson's r employed?
11 How are correlation coefficients interpreted? Name the main trends that can be identified in a correlation coefficient.
12 When, under what conditions and for what purpose is regression employed?

Definitions of concepts

Define the following concepts:

Coefficient of determination

....

Correlation

....

Gamma (γ)

....

Lambda (λ)

....

Negative correlation

....

Pearson's r

....

Positive correlation

....

Prediction

....

Regression

....

Sommer's *d*

....

Spearman's rho (ρ)

....

Yule's *Q*

....

Zero correlation

....

Practical exercises

1   In a recent study, 1500 males and females of the same age group (in equal
    numbers) were asked to state their educational status by indicating whether
    they had attended tertiary institutions or not. The findings are given in the fol-
    lowing table:

Educational status	Tertiary	No tertiary	Total
Males	612	220	832
Females	138	530	668
Total	750	750	1500

Use Yule's *Q* to estimate the relationship between tertiary studies and gender.

2   In an interview of spouses, husbands and wives ranked the five political
    parties presented to them as follows:

Parties	Husband's ranking	Wife's ranking	D	D²
Liberal	1	2		
Labour	5	4		
National	2	1		
Country	3	3		
Democrats	4	5		

Compute Spearman's rho to estimate the relationship between the variables in question (try manually first).

3   Students of group C of the History class were asked to state how many hours they studied the day before the last test. Their responses were collated with the test scores (1 to 10), both of which are given below:

Student:	A	B	C	D	E	F	G	H	I	J	K	L	M	N	O
Hours:	4	6	8	9	5	2	5	9	6	7	6	4	7	6	9
Score:	6	8	6	5	6	4	7	4	4	8	5	6	9	4	7

Can you assert that there is a correlation between hours of study and test performance? More specifically, can you argue that the more students studied before the examination, the more likely it is for them to achieve a high test score?

Use Pearson's correlation coefficient to test this hypothesis.

➧ Firstly, enter the data in the computer, setting them in two columns, one for study time (hours), and one for scores.

➧ Then, construct a scattergram to obtain a visual presentation of the relationship between these two variables. To do this, proceed as follows:

a Choose Charts>Scatter
b Click on **Simple**
c Click on **Define**
d Transfer 'Hours' to **Y Axis**
e Transfer 'Scores' to **X Axis**
f Click **OK**

Examine the scattergram; what does it tell you about the relationship between hours of study and test result? Is there a relationship? If so, is it strong/weak, positive/negative?

➧ Now compute Pearson's *r* to explore the relationship between the variables in question and to see whether the conclusion drawn on the basis of this computation is consistent with the indication given by the scattergram. Proceed as follows:

a Choose Statistics>Summarise>Crosstabs
b Transfer 'Scores' to **Rows** box
c Transfer 'Hours' to **Columns** box
d Click on **Statistics** at the bottom of the window
e Click on ☐ in front of **Correlations**
f Click on **Continue**
g Click on **OK**

➟ What conclusion can you draw from the findings?

➟ How consistent is the correlation coefficient with the shape of the scattergram?

4   Among other things, a study of marital power explored two issues: the degree to which spouses accepted the power system of their marriage and the degree of marital satisfaction. The question here was about whether high acceptance of the power system of marriage was associated with high marital satisfaction. The answers of the first 10 respondents to these two questions are given below. Scores range from 1 (low) to 9 (high):

Spouse:	A	B	C	D	E	F	G	H	I	J
Acceptance:	7	8	5	7	4	6	8	3	7	6
Satisfaction:	8	9	4	6	5	7	7	2	8	6

➟ Construct a scattergram. What can be concluded on the basis of its structure?

➟ Compute Pearson's r. What can be concluded about the relationship between acceptance of marital power and marital satisfaction?

➟ How consistent are the findings of the scattergram and Pearson's correlation coefficient?

18

Tests of significance

Contents

Educational objectives

After completing this chapter, you will:

1 have an understanding of the nature and purpose of significance tests in social research;

2   be aware of the strengths and limitations of significance tests;
3   be in a position to differentiate between the various tests that are employed in particular types of data;
4   be able to interpret results of tests of significance;
5   be in a position to choose the right tests and apply them as required;
6   have a critical understanding of the limitations of these tests and their place in social research.

Main points

The main points made in this chapter are:

1   Tests of significance relate statistics to parameters; the sample to the target population; the study to the society.
2   Statistics are attributes of the sample; parameters are attributes of the population.
3   The choice of tests of significance depends on type of measurement, number of samples, and dependence or independence of the samples.
4   One-tail tests assume that parameters are different in a specific way, showing the direction of the difference; one-tail tests are directional.
5   Two-tail tests assume that parameters are just different (without showing the direction of difference). They are non-directional.
6   Parametric tests assume that the variable in question is normally distributed in the population; they employ the normal curve.
7   Non-parametric tests do not assume that the variable is normally distributed in the population.
8   Tests of significance work around the notion of null hypothesis (Ho): if the significance level of a particular test is below .05, the Ho is rejected; if it is above .05, the Ho is accepted.
9   The most common test of significance for nominally measured data is the chi-square test.
10   There are two types of chi-square tests: the goodness-of-fit test and the test of independence.
11   The goodness-of-fit test examines the extent to which collected data are close to typical cases, that is, close to what is expected; it therefore compares observed with expected frequencies.
12   The test of independence examines – as the name indicates – whether the two variables are independent from each other.
13   The z-test is a test of significance employed when data is expressed in proportions.
14   Ordinal-level tests of significance are less common in social sciences than other tests.
15   Two of the most common tests of significance for interval/ratio level data are the *t*-test and ANOVA.
16   The *t*-test and ANOVA compare means rather than scores. They answer the question whether the differences between the means are significant or not.
17   The *t*-test is a parametric test and is employed when one or two (dependent or independent) samples are considered.

18 ANOVA is similar to the *t*-test except that it can test more than two variables concurrently.
19 ANOVA is employed under the assumption that scores are independent from each other, that they are normally distributed and that variances are equal.
20 Computer programs such as SPSS can assist with computing significance tests, making relevant computations and conclusions fast, precise and easy.

Short-answer questions

Answer each question carefully. Consult your Social Research *text when your memory fails you or when you are in doubt about the accuracy of your responses.*

1   What are tests of significance and what is their purpose?
2   What is a one-tailed and what is a two-tailed test?
3   What are parametric and what non-parametric tests?
4   What are the main significance tests that are suitable for nominal-level data?
5   What are chi-square tests and what is their purpose?
6   What is a goodness-of-fit test and for what purpose is it employed?
7   How are the chi-square results interpreted?
8   When is a chi-square test of independence employed and for what purpose?
9   How are findings of a chi-square test of independence interpreted?
10 What is characteristic about the *z*-test, when is it employed and how are the findings interpreted?
11 What is characteristic about the *t*-test, when is it employed and how are the findings interpreted?
12 What are the types of *t*-tests and when are they used in social research?
13 Explain the purpose of ANOVA test and the way in which *F* is interpreted.

Definitions of concepts

Define the following concepts:

Analysis of variance

....

Cochran's *Q*-test

....

Fisher's exact test

....

Friedman test

....

Interval ratio level tests

....

Kolmogorov-Smirnov test

Kruskal-Wallis *H*-test

Mann-Whitney test

McNemar test

Nominal-level tests

Non-parametric tests

One-tail tests

One-way analysis of variance

Ordinal-level tests

Parametric tests

Sign test

Tests of significance

t-test

Two-tail tests

Two-way analysis of variance

....

Wald-Wolfowitz runs test

....

Wilcoxon test

....

χ^2 goodness-of-fit test

....

χ^2 test

....

χ^2 test of independence

....

z-test

....

z-test for proportions

....

Practical exercises

1   Of the 380 students who were admitted to the Bachelor of Arts this year, 120 decided to major in psychology, 135 in History, and 125 in sociology. Is there a significant difference between these preferences?

To answer this question, employ the goodness-of-fit χ^2 test. To compute the χ^2 value, and to estimate its level of significance, employ SPSS.

First of all, enter the data in the computer. Use 1 for those choosing psychology as a major, 2 for those choosing history and 3 for those choosing sociology; enter 120 times the digit 1, 135 times the digit 2, and 125 times the digit 3, all in one column.

Having set the data in the computer, under the name 'Majors', proceed as follows:

a   Choose Statistics>Nonparametric tests>Chi-square
b   Transfer 'Majors' to the **Test Variable** box

c   Activate (click on **O** in front of) **All categories equal**
d   Click on OK

The computer displays the results. You have to identify first the χ^2 value and then the significance level. Remember, if the figure given under the label 'Significance' is larger than .05, the differences are not significant.

What is the computer level of significance? What can you conclude from that? What is the null hypothesis (Ho)? Can you reject the Ho?

2   A study of same-sex and other-sex couples revealed that degree of commitment (high, low) to their relationship is as follows:

Couples	High degree	Low degree	Total
Same-sex	65	42	107
Other-sex	57	50	107
Total	122	92	224

On the basis of these figures, what can be said about the level of commitment of these two groups of couples? Are the differences in commitment between these two groups significant?

Remember, first enter the data in the computer using the tabular method. Here the data will be set in three columns, as shown below:

1	1	65
1	2	42
2	1	57
2	2	50

Call the variables, 'Couples', 'Commitm' and 'Count'. The first two variables have the values 1 and 2. The latter requires no values. The steps that follow are simple:

a   Choose Statistics>Summarize>Crosstabs
b   Transfer 'Commitm' to the **Rows** box
c   Transfer 'Couples' to the **Column** box
d   Choose Data>Weight cases
e   Activate **Weight cases by** box
f   Transfer 'Count' to the **Frequency variable** box
g   Click on OK
h   Click on **Statistics**
i   Click on ☐ in front of **Chi-square** box
j   Click on OK
k   Click on OK

What is the χ^2 value? What is the Ho? At what level are the differences significant? Can you reject the Ho? What can you say about the differences on commitment for the two couple groups?

3   In the above example, compute the ϕ coefficient and Cramer's *V*. What can you conclude from these findings?

4   A family researcher knows that the proportion of childless heterosexual couples having a dog at home is 12 per cent. In a study of same-sex couples, this researcher found that the proportion of childless couples having a dog at home is 18 per cent. Can you say from this that the proportion of same-sex childless couples who have dogs is larger than that of heterosexual couples (that is, that the differences are significant)?

Use the *z*-test to answer this question.

5   In a recent study, 25 farm wives were interviewed to determine the level of satisfaction they had with their marriage. Rated between, 1 (very low) and 9 (very high), their responses were as follows: 4.5, 5.3, 6.1, 6.3, 5.8, 8.3, 7.8, 5.6, 8.1, 6.8, 6.4, 6.1, 6.3, 5.9, 5.6, 4.4, 6.6, 7.4, 6.6, 5.7, 5.5, 7.3, 6.7, 7.4, 6.3. Knowing that the average marital satisfaction score among city wives is 6.2, what can you conclude from this study?

Use a one-sample *t*-test here. Remember to set the scores in one column. You may name it 'Satisf' for satisfaction. The steps are as follows:

a   Choose Statistics>Compare means>one-sample *t*-Test
b   Transfer 'Satisf' to the **Test variable(s)** box
c   Type 6.2 in the box next to **Test value**
d   Click OK

Remember that you are comparing means here. What is the Ho? What is the *t*-value? Taking into consideration these results, can you reject Ho? What can you say about the level of satisfaction of farm wives?

6   The same 25 farm wives referred to above were interviewed together with 25 city wives. The purpose of the interview was to ascertain the amount of time (hours) spent by wives with their husband per day. The results of the questioning are given below:

City wives: 3, 2, 3, 3, 4, 3, 2, 1, 2, 1, 2, 5, 6, 5, 4, 7, 6, 4, 5, 6, 3, 5, 4, 3, 5
Farm wives: 4, 3, 4, 4, 5, 4, 3, 2, 3, 2, 3, 6, 7, 6, 5, 7, 7, 5, 6, 7, 4, 6, 5, 4, 7

Is the difference between the responses of the two groups significant?

To answer this question, employ a *t*-test. The computation of the *t*-value is similar to that of Example H in the *Social Research* text, with the difference that here you use place of residence instead of gender. The other variable (hours) is the same. Remember, in *t*-tests you compare the means, and employ a null hypothesis (Ho) which you intend to test. What is the Ho? Can you reject the Ho?

7   Three groups of students (N = 20 each), one from a large city, one from a small town and one from a remote area were tested to determine their overall scholastic achievement. The students were matched according to social and family background. The scores of the three groups are shown below.

Scores by group of respondents

City	Town	Remote
5	6	6
6	7	8
7	8	6
5	6	9
6	7	5
4	5	6
5	7	3
4	9	5
6	8	4
5	7	6
7	8	3
6	6	4
5	7	2
6	8	4
4	7	3
7	9	5
5	6	4
6	7	6
5	5	5
4	6	8

Are the differences between the scores of the three groups of students significant? Can you say that students' results vary according to their place of residence? Obviously, ANOVA will help you answer these questions. Here you compare means and you set a null hypothesis (Ho). The results of the ANOVA will tell you whether you accept or reject the Ho.

What often confuses students is how to set the data in the computer. When everything is in place, the steps to follow are simple and straightforward. So you have to pay attention to this. How then do you set the data in the computer?

Here you follow the same steps you followed in Example J in the *Social Research* text. The variables are 'Scores' (dependent variable) and 'Groups' (independent variable or factor). The groups are numbered 1 (city students), 2 (town students) and 3 (remote students). You then set each student's score in one column, followed by the student's group set in the second column.

The steps to take from there are as follows:

    a Choose Statistics>Compare means> One-way ANOVA
    b Transfer 'Scores' to the **Dependent list** box
    c Transfer 'Groups' to the **Factor** box
    d Click on **Define range**
    e Type 1 in the **Minimum** box, and 5 in the **Maximum** box
    f Click on **Continue**
    g Click on **OK**

What is the F-ratio? What is the F-probability? What can you say about the research question? Can you reject the null hypothesis?

19

Reporting

Contents

Educational objectives

After completing this chapter, you will:

1 have an understanding of the ways in which research findings are reported;
2 be able to distinguish between the methods of reporting employed in quantitative and qualitative research;
3 be aware of the political elements that influence the process of publication of findings in social sciences;
4 be in a position to compile a research report in both contexts, the quantitative and the qualitative context;

5   be able to critically evaluate the methodological soundness of reports published at the various levels and outlets.

Main points

The main points made in this chapter are:

1   Reporting relates to the dissemination of the information collected through the study.
2   Of the factors that affect the writing of the report, ethical considerations, the reader and the purpose of the report are most important.
3   The most common outlets of the results of a study are newspapers, newsletters, conferences, monographs, journal articles and books.
4   The structure of the report varies with the type and nature of publication.
5   The main parts of a report are the abstract, introduction, method, results, discussion, conclusion, recommendation and references. Some of these parts are optional.
6   The criteria that mark a good report are clarity, precision, legibility, completeness, objectivity, fairness, verifiability, impersonality and ethics.
7   With regard to presentation, consideration must be given to whether to use the first or third person, active or passive voice, and past or present tense, and to the type of language. Requirements for the type of language are stated firmly in the *Social Research* text but the other points are open to discussion.
8   Manuscripts should be subjected to vigorous self-assessment before they are submitted for publication.
9   The structure of a book may be similar to that of other reports but consideration must be given to its nature, scope and size.
10   The politics of publishing constitutes a very important factor and requires adequate consideration.

Short-answer questions

Answer each question carefully. Consult your Social Research *text when your memory fails you or when you are in doubt about the accuracy of your responses.*

1   What are the main elements or areas of a report?
2   What issues are expected to be considered in 'The method' section of a report?
3   What should 'The findings' section of a report contain?
4   What are some of the issues that are expected to be considered in 'The discussion' section of a report?
5   List the major standards of presentation that must be considered when preparing a research report.
6   What are some of the issues considered when assessing a report? Refer to all report parts in succession.
7   What are the most common models of structure employed when presenting the findings in a book form?